MICROSOFT®
WINDOWS MEDIA™
PLAYER 7
HANDBOOK

SETH McEVOY

PUBLISHED BY
Microsoft Press
A Division of Microsoft Corporation
One Microsoft Way
Redmond, Washington 98052-6399

Library of Congress Cataloging-in-Publication Data
McEvoy, Seth.
    Microsoft Windows Media Player Handbook / Seth McEvoy.
       p. cm.
    Includes index.
    ISBN 0-7356-1178-5
    1. Interactive multimedia.   2. Microsoft Windows (Computer file).   I. Title.

   QA76.76.I59 M335   2000
   006.6--dc21   00-056229

Printed and bound in the United States of America.

1 2 3 4 5 6 7 8 9   QWT   5 4 3 2 1 0

Distributed in Canada by Penguin Books Canada Limited.

A CIP catalogue record for this book is available from the British Library.

Microsoft Press books are available through booksellers and distributors worldwide. For further information about international editions, contact your local Microsoft Corporation office or contact Microsoft Press International directly at fax (425) 936-7329. Visit our Web site at mspress.microsoft.com. Send comments to mspinput@microsoft.com.

Acquisitions Editor: Casey Doyle
Project Editors: Denise Bankaitis and Victoria Thulman

To my wife, Laure Smith, without whom none of this would have been possible.

Contents

Introduction

Playing music and video on your computer will be better than ever with the new Microsoft Windows Media Player 7. The latest features of the Player will make it even easier to get the entertainment you want when you want it. You can still play audio and video files like you did with previous versions of Windows Media Player, but now you can do so much more. You'll have more access to the Internet, more flexibility of files and formats, and you can even change the look and functionality of your Player. Here is a summary of the major new features in version 7:

Media Library

Windows Media Player now includes **Media Library**, which lets you create multiple playlists to organize all your audio and video files. You can also use it to search your computer or network drives for new audio and video to add to your collection.

Media Guide

The Player opens up a window to the Internet with its new **Media Guide**, which provides daily entertainment news, free downloads, and live, streaming audio and video.

CD Audio

The Player's new **CD Audio** feature lets you copy tracks from a CD and convert them to compressed Windows Media files, turning your computer into a giant jukebox. You can also make new CDs from music on your computer with just a few easy steps.

Skins

Windows Media Player's revolutionary new skin technology means that the user interface for the Player is now completely changeable. A skin is the Player's new customizable user interface that can change not only how the Player looks, but how it operates. You can create your own skin designs or choose from those available on the Internet or on this book's companion CD.

Visualizations

The Player will now entertain you with visual images that dance along with the music. This new feature is called visualizations, and their animated lights, colors, and shapes move in time to the tone and rhythm.

Radio Tuner

The new **Radio Tuner** can listen to Internet radio stations from around the globe 24 hours a day. There are hundreds of different stations that broadcast everything from news to talk shows to every imaginable style of music. Plus, the tuner lets you search for stations by category.

Portable Device

The **Portable Device** feature makes it easy to download music to the Pocket PC computer and other portable music devices, enabling you to carry your own personal music selections anywhere.

Who is this book for?

This book is designed for all levels of computer experience, from the novice to the expert professional, including end users, artists, designers, and developers. The three parts of this book are tailored for the different needs of each audience.

End user

Part 1 of this book is the only section the end user will need. It includes installation procedures and instructions for using Windows Media Player 7. It also covers the concepts of digital audio and video multimedia, so you can gain a greater understanding of what the Player does and why.

Designer

This book explains how to design and build skins. Creating art for skins is very similar to creating art for Web pages. You don't need to know how to draw or paint, but you do need to be able to use an art program such as Adobe Photoshop. The programming technologies used in skin creation are XML, which is similar to HTML, and Microsoft JScript, which is similar to Perl and other scripting languages.

Developer

If you want to use Windows Media Player to develop advanced applications, you'll need experience with Web programming technologies such as HTML, ActiveX , and JScript. In Part 3, you will find out how to make Web pages more interactive with Windows Media Player, and how to modify media files to include markers, URLs, and script commands. You will also learn how to create multimedia advertisements that can be packaged with audio and video files to promote your Web site, music CDs, or other products. Finally, if you are a C++ programmer, you can learn how to create visualizations that you can use to enhance skins.

How this book is organized

This book is divided into three parts. The first part covers how to install and use the Player. Creating skins is the focus of the second part. The third part covers advanced programming topic such as Web page programming, creating advertisements, and visualizations. In addition, this book has a companion CD that contains a copy of Windows Media Player 7, sample skins and visualizations, the Windows Media 7 SDK, and more.

Part 1: Using Windows Media Player

The first part of this book has five chapters that cover what you need to know to use Windows Media Player, including explanations of all the features. Because it includes information on the many features that are new to Windows Media Player 7, this part is for all users. Here is what is in each chapter:

Chapter 1 introduces the basic concepts of Windows Media Player. A complete guide to installing the Player is provided. This chapter also includes detailed information on installing skins and visualizations.

Chapter 2 explains all the major features and how to use the Player. It covers every option, menu item, and task available to the user. You'll learn how to use the **Media Guide** to find new music and how the **Media Library** can keep track of all your music and video and organize it into playlists. You'll learn how to access Internet radio stations using the **Radio Tuner**, download music to your portable computer or music player using the **Portable Device** feature, and copy music from music CDs to your computer using the **CD Audio** feature.

Chapter 3 discusses the file formats that the Player can use, as well as information on how to create your own CDs. You'll learn more about encoding music and be introduced to the world of codecs. Digital rights are important to users of Internet music, and you'll learn how the Player addresses this issue.

Chapter 4 covers the Internet audio and video revolution and shows you how to download files and receive live, streaming audio and video. Networking concepts are explained, as well as the different ways that streaming media work to bring audio and video to your computer. This chapter will compare the concepts of file downloading, progressive file downloading, and streaming.

Chapter 5 tells you more about how to use the **Portable Device** feature to copy music to a Pocket PC or portable music device. You will also learn how to use the Pocket PC version of Windows Media Player.

Part 2: Creating Skins

The second part of this book is all about skins. It's directed at the artists, designers, and developers who want to create art and programming code for skins. Included are step-by-step instructions that cover the entire process. Here is what is in each chapter:

Chapter 6 introduces the unique architecture of skins, and shows you how artwork, XML, and JScript work together to make a skin. You'll get tips on how to create your own artwork and suggestions on how to learn from other people's skins.

Chapter 7 discusses the concepts of skin design and suggests a process to follow. You'll find user interface guidelines and a procedure for skin design that will help you fit together all the aspects of skin art and skin programming.

Chapter 8 walks you through the step-by-step process of creating a simple skin. You will learn how to choose the functionality you want, design the user interface, create the art, and write the programming code.

Chapter 9 builds on Chapter 8 by showing you how to add more functionality to a skin with progress bars, sliders, custom sliders, and predefined buttons. You will learn how to add video, visualizations, playlists, and other user-interface elements to a skin.

Chapter 10 provides details on how to test skins. You'll be shown testing techniques that will help you create better skins, and guidelines on what problems to look for. You'll also learn how to submit your skins for distribution on Microsoft's Skin Gallery Web site.

Part 3: Advanced Topics

The third part of this book is primarily for developers and will cover advanced topics such as using Windows Media Player in a Web page, modifying audio and video for Web page programming, creating interactive multimedia advertisements for the Player, and programming visualizations. Here is what is in each chapter:

Chapter 11 shows you how to add audio and video to Web pages by using the Windows Media Player ActiveX control. You will learn how you can embed the Player in a Web page and take advantage of all the functionality that Internet Explorer provides.

Chapter 12 discusses the tools and techniques needed to create special audio and video files that you can use to create interactive programs that actively involve the viewer. You'll learn how to embed markers in a media file so that the user can jump to a specific location in the program. You'll see how to add URLs (links) to files so that Web pages will be displayed while the program is playing. You'll also be shown how to modify audio and video files with custom commands so that your Web page programming can take full advantage of the Player's core features.

Chapter 13 covers the techniques of adding advertisements to downloadable media. You will see how to customize Windows Media Player to link your message to specific songs and videos. You can create "click here to buy" portions of a skin and embed audio or video within a skin to create interactive advertising. The Player gives you all the tools to combine audio, video, custom user interfaces, and the Internet into one package, so you can also use these same techniques to create full multimedia applications.

Chapter 14 explains how to create custom visualizations. You'll see how the tools of Windows programming and C++ work together to create your own visual images that will move in time to the music. You'll also learn how to create a simple visualization using the Visualization Wizard.

What's on the companion CD?

This book includes a companion CD-ROM that gives you tools and more information to help you create skins, Web pages, and visualizations. The CD contains the following items.

Windows Media Player 7

If you don't have it and you don't want to download it, get it here.

Windows Media Player 7 SDK

This contains tutorial and reference information on how to create skins, visualizations, and Web pages. It also includes the Visualization Wizard and more than a dozen working sample skins and Web pages.

Windows Media Player for Palm-size and Pocket PC Skin Development Kit

The Windows Media Player for Palm-size and Pocket PC skin Development Kit includes everything you need to create skins for a Palm-size or a Pocket PC.

Windows Media Advanced Script Indexer

This software tool can be used to insert markers, URLs, and script commands into an audio or video file, as well as change the title, author, and other text information that is embedded in the file.

Windows Media Player 7 PowerToys

The Microsoft Windows Media Player 7 team has put together a set of utilities called PowerToys. These are add-ons and other utilities that enhance Windows Media Player 7. PowerToys are not supported, so Microsoft Technical Support won't be able to answer any questions about them.

Featured skins

You can install additional skins that were created just for this book, such as Cubist, Goldfish Bowl, and Deco.

Additional skins

Several other skins available on the Internet are included so you won't have to download them.

Skin Construction Kit

An assortment of buttons, sliders, and backgrounds is provided so you can use them in your own skins. The kit also includes samples of source code that you can cut and paste for your own use.

ActiveSync for Palm-size and Pocket PCs

This section includes instructions and files needed to use ActiveSync and the Skin Chooser tools. These tools are required to install skins for Windows Media Player for Pocket PCs and Palm-size PCs.

Skins for Palm-size and Pocket PCs

These skins let you personalize Windows Media Player for Pocket PC and Palm-size PC.

Audio and Video Content

Although we know you will want to surf the Web and accumulate your own "library" of media files to play through your Windows Media Player 7; we supplied some audio and video content for you.

Tutorials

Additional tutorials on creating skins are provided to demonstrate how to create skins using Microsoft PhotoDraw and Paint. These tutorials also include art, .wms files, and everything else you need to create a fully functional skin.

Visualizations

Visualizations available on the Internet are included so you won't have to download them.

Tips & Tricks

Several tips and tricks are included to teach you some of the lesser-known features of the Windows Media Player 7.

The companion CD requires one of the following operating systems:

- Microsoft Windows 98 or Windows 98 Second Edition
- Microsoft Windows NT Server version 4.0 with Service Pack 6
- Microsoft Windows NT Workstation version 4.0 with Service Pack 6
- Microsoft Windows 2000 Professional or Windows 2000 Server
- Microsoft Windows Millennium Edition

In addition, the following is required for some portions of the companion CD:

- Microsoft Internet Explorer 5.0 or later

The information provided in this book is that which was available on the date of publication and may change.

Acknowledgments

This book could not have been done without the invaluable contributions of many talented people. Their insight, enthusiasm, and hard work made it possible to put this book together in record time. I am extremely grateful to each and every person.

I want to extend an extra-special thank you to the technical editor, Steve Hug, for his Herculean effort and careful attention to detail. He literally worked around the clock, tirelessly combing over every word, screen shot, and line of code. C. Keith Gabbert and Tom Woolums did an amazing job of pulling together the contents of the companion CD, making it easy and fun to use. Without Greg Lovitt's skillful conversion of the text and artwork, this book would never have made it to the printer. I want to extend my appreciation to Denise Bankaitis, project editor at Microsoft Press, for coordinating everything with such efficiency, intelligence, and understanding.

In addition, I am grateful to the outstanding contributions of the following people: Geoff Harris for technically reviewing the entire book; Mark Galioto for the technical review of Chapter 4; Thomas Thornton for the technical review of Chapter 5; Nadja Vol-Ochs Wilson for the technical review of Chapter 8; Josh Cain for the technical review of Chapter 10; Dave Fester for helping with cover questions and other marketing issues; Zach Robinson for some helpful ActiveX test code; David Wrede for writing the documentation for Windows Media Advanced Script Indexer; Ned Cannon (of Ned Cannon Illustration & Design) for creating the artwork for the Skin Construction Kit, the Cubist, Deco, and Goldfish skins, and the futuristic Web page design in Chapter 11; Stephen Beecroft and John Shaw for writing the Ovoid tutorial and creating the code for the Skin Construction Kit; Matt Lichtenberg for writing the Radial tutorial; John Green, Henry Bale, Robert "Bob" Porter, and Cornel Moiceanu for their testing, coding and general help to the CD effort; Cornel also created the extended dance music on the CD; Kelly Pittman, David M. Nelson, Dagmar Shannon, Gail McClellan, John Shaw, Tricia Gill, Andrea Pruneda, Mark Galioto, Sharon Carroll, and Terrence Dorsey for general proofreading of the chapters; Terrence also did the indexing of the whole book; Donna Corey, Sue Glueck, Glenn Schroeder, and Laura Heisler for doing legal reviews of the chapters; Karen Strudwick for editorial help; and special thanks to Casey Doyle and Victoria Thulman at Microsoft Press for getting this book started.

Microsoft Press support information

Every effort has been made to ensure the accuracy of the book and the contents of this companion CD. Microsoft Press provides corrections for books through the World Wide Web at:

http://mspress.microsoft.com/support/

If you have comments, questions, or ideas regarding the book or this companion CD, please send them to Microsoft Press via e-mail to:

MSPInput@Microsoft.com

or via postal mail to:

Microsoft Press
Attn: Microsoft Windows Media Player 7 Handbook Editor
One Microsoft Way
Redmond, WA 98052-6399

Please note that product support is not offered through the above addresses.

Part 1
Using Windows Media Player

CHAPTER 1

Getting Started

This chapter will introduce you to the basic features of Microsoft Windows Media Player 7. Detailed explanations of all the installation procedures are also provided, including how to install two new types of enhancements to the Player, skins and visualizations. In later chapters, you'll learn more about each feature, and how you can use them to customize the look and functionality of the Player.

What is Windows Media Player?

One of the best places to learn about new music and videos is through the Internet. A world of entertainment and education is out there, and Windows Media Player can help you navigate the Web to find exactly what you want. Then you can use the Player to download it, customize it, and play it on your computer or Pocket PC.

You're likely to have a CD-ROM drive in your computer. With it, Windows Media Player can play a music CD and let you choose your favorite songs. The Player can also copy music from your CDs to your computer, so you can file and play the music any way you want to.

After copying or downloading your audio and video files, you can keep track of what's stored on your computer. Windows Media Player has a media library that can help you organize all of your media selections. You can create specific playlists that combine your songs and movies however you like. Keep all your classical music in one playlist and your jazz in another. Or have a different playlist for every day of the week!

Basically, Windows Media Player is the computer equivalent of other media-playing devices such as radio, television, and CD players. The big difference is that Windows Media Player is a software product that makes it possible to see video and hear audio on your computer, but it's even more than that. The Player allows you to design your own entertainment experience. Not only can the Player read an assortment of live and recorded media formats, but it can organize your files, search for specific kinds of audio and video, copy music to other devices, and enhance Web pages. In addition, you can create custom visual elements with unique animated effects.

Here are the main features of Windows Media Player 7:

Now Playing: plays music and video

The **Now Playing** feature is the main user interface for Windows Media Player and controls the basic functions of the Player. It starts and stops the sound and images, adjusts the bass and treble, and fast forwards or rewinds. This feature can also play audio and video in several file formats, including Windows Media format (WMA, WMV, ASF), WAV, AVI, and MP3.

Media Library: organizes your files

The new **Media Library** feature can help you organize your music into specific categories. This feature lets you combine your music into lists called *playlists* that you can rearrange the way you want. Playlists enable you to create your own sequences of music and video and make your own customized CDs. If you don't like the order of the songs on a CD, you can reorganize them and keep only the songs you like.

Media Guide: searches the Internet

Media Guide can help you find new music and videos on the Internet. This new feature enables you to access streaming audio and video, entertainment news, and links to media Web sites. You can also connect to the latest Internet radio sites, download music files tailored to the speed of your modem, and watch broadband videos.

CD Audio: copies music from CDs

If you have a CD player on your computer, the new **CD Audio** feature can copy the tracks from your music CDs to the hard disk. You can then create customized playlists from several CDs, combining your favorite music. With this feature, you can create a music collection on your computer and keep your CDs in their cases so they won't get scratched or dusty.

If you have a CD recorder, the **CD Audio** feature can take a playlist and make a brand new CD for you. Recording tracks onto a blank CD is called *burning*. With the **CD Audio** feature, you can put music in a playlist, burn a new CD, and listen to it on any standard CD player.

Skin Chooser: provides custom user interfaces

Windows Media Player can now be customized with visual elements called *skins*. A skin is a graphical user interface on your computer screen that replaces the original buttons, sliders, and windows of the Player with new artwork. The new **Skin Chooser** feature makes it possible for you to apply new skin artwork to your player. If you don't like the way the Player looks, download a new look, or create your own skin that has a user interface that you like better.

Figures 1.1a, 1.1b, and 1.1c show some skins that are included with Windows Media Player.

Figure 1.1a – *Toothy skin.*

Figure 1.1b – *Headspace skin.*

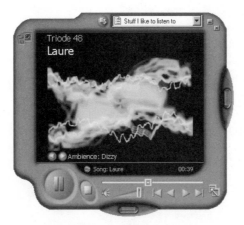

Figure 1.1c – *Default skin.*

Visualizations: dance to the music

If you're watching a video on Windows Media Player, you have a moving image to look at. But if you're listening to music without a video, the Player can create moving images, called *visualizations*. The new visualization feature can create light, color, and patterns that move in time to the music. This imagery is similar to the way that an oscilloscope reacts to sound waves.

Figures 1.2a, 1.2b, and 1.2c show some of the visualizations that are included with the Player.

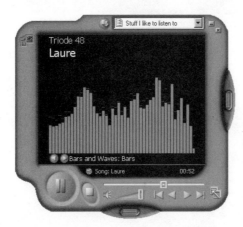

Figure 1.2a – *Bars and Waves visualization with the Bars preset.*

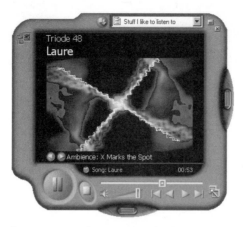

Figure 1.2b – *Ambience visualization with the X Marks the Spot preset.*

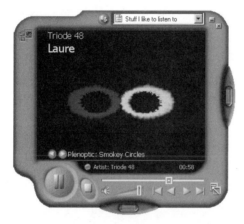

Figure 1.2c – *Plenoptic visualization with the Smokey Circles preset.*

Portable Device: copies music to your pocket

Computers don't always fit in your pocket. If you want to listen to music while you're on the go, the new **Portable Device** feature of the Player can take music from your computer and easily transfer it to a portable music player, such as the Pocket PC, the Creative NOMAD, the S3 Rio, and others. This process takes only a few simple steps. You can also monitor how much space is available on your portable device, and remove audio files from your device if you need more space.

Radio Tuner: tune in to Internet radio

Using the new **Radio Tuner** feature, you can listen to Internet radio stations from around the globe. Whatever your taste in music or interest in current events, you can find a radio station that will suit your needs. The **Station Finder** helps you search by category, language, or location.

Installing Windows Media Player

You can always get the latest version of the Player at the Microsoft Windows Media Web site:

http://www.windowsmedia.com/

At the Web site, follow the directions for downloading Windows Media Player. You can choose whether to download the installation file first or install the Player directly from the Web. If you have a good connection, you can install it from the Web, but you'll be safer if you download the installation file to your computer first and then start the installation from there. If your Internet connection drops in the middle of an installation, you might have to repeat the whole process.

If you have a previous version of Windows Media Player, you'll want to upgrade to the latest version because you won't want to miss out on skins, visualizations, and the many other improvements that Windows Media Player 7 includes.

If you have Windows Millennium installed on your computer, you don't need to install Windows Media Player 7 because it is included with the operating system. You can still customize it by selecting **Options** from the **Tools** menu.

Beginning your installation

When you install Windows Media Player 7, you are shown a series of dialog boxes and asked a few questions. One of the best features of the Player is that you can customize which components you want to include in your personal configuration. If you don't want to customize your Player when you install it, choose the default options. This will make your installation quick and easy. If you want to customize the functionality of your Player, select the exact features you want in each dialog box.

The dialog boxes will appear in the following sequence:

Closing other applications

When the installation begins, you will be shown a dialog box similar to Figure 1.3.

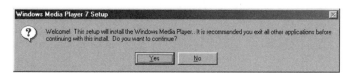

Figure 1.3 – *Windows Media Player 7 Setup dialog box.*

This dialog box welcomes you to the installation process and then recommends that you exit all other applications before continuing. You should close any other applications that you don't need to have running; otherwise the Player may not be able to complete the installation correctly. It is most important to close any other audio or video applications that are running. You can look at the task bar to see if anything is running that you might want to close. If you have an application that should not be shut down, the Player can probably work around it. Windows Media Player is not easily confused, but you don't want to make it harder than necessary for the Player to detect the hardware and software on your computer.

If you can't close your other applications now, you can say no to the Player installation dialog box, and then start the installation again at a time when you can close your other applications.

Agreeing to the license

After you have closed other applications, the next dialog box you'll see looks like Figure 1.4.

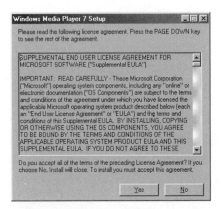

Figure 1.4 – *The End User License Agreement (EULA).*

You'll be asked whether you accept the End User License Agreement (EULA). If you don't accept it, you can't go on. The agreement outlines the terms under which you can use Windows Media Player. You should scroll down to read the rest of the agreement.

Watching the files unpack

After you accept the license, files are extracted from the installation package. You can watch the progress bar in a dialog box that looks like Figure 1.5.

Figure 1.5 – *Extracting files.*

Usually you'll want to extract all the files, but if you need to cancel the installation at this point, you can click the **Cancel** button to stop the process.

Starting the setup

After the files are extracted and copied to a temporary location on your computer, you're ready for the setup phase, where you can choose the configuration of your Player. The dialog box welcoming you to component setup looks like Figure 1.6.

Figure 1.6 – *Component setup.*

You can cancel the setup at this point, but if you want to continue, click the
Next button.

Reading the Privacy Statement

Before you can begin component installation, you'll be shown a statement
about the information the Player can share on the Internet or over a network.
The dialog box containing the Privacy Statement looks like Figure 1.7.

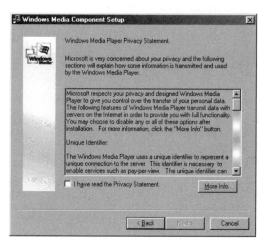

Figure 1.7 – *Privacy Statement.*

You must read the statement in order to continue with the installation. Each part of the Privacy Statement covers a specific technology that involves privacy. The statement tells you what the technology is and how to disable it later if you do not want to share specific information. If you are connected to the Internet, you can click the **More Info** button for information that will explain more about the privacy issues.

After you have read the Privacy Statement, select the check box, indicating that you have read the Privacy Statement. Note that you are not agreeing to share or not share information over the Internet at this point in the installation. If you want to change privacy options, you must change them after the installation is complete. After selecting the check box, the **Next** button appears. Click it to continue the installation.

Upgrading new components only

Next you'll see a dialog box that asks you whether you want to install all of the components of Windows Media Player or just the new ones. The dialog box looks like Figure 1.8.

Figure 1.8 – *Upgrading new components only.*

If you are installing over a slow connection, you might want to install only components that are newer than the ones already on your computer. Installing all components will take longer but is safer because you know that all the components the Player needs will be installed properly.

When you've made your choice, click **Next** to continue. You can always click **Cancel** to quit the installation process, or **Back** if you suddenly realize you made a mistake on a previous dialog box.

Choosing components

You are next asked which components you want to install. Figure 1.9 shows the dialog box for making these choices.

You will probably want to install all the components on your computer, unless you are low on hard disk space. If you're not sure about a particular component, click the text of each option and a paragraph will appear on the lower portion of the dialog box explaining what the option does. If an option says, "This component must be installed for the software to function," then you should install it.

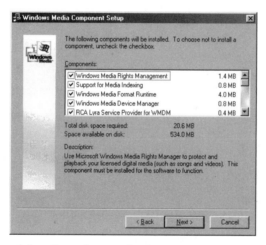

Figure 1.9 – *Specifying which components to install.*

Many of the components you can install are called *codecs*. You will probably want to install all the codecs in the list, because codecs provide information to help the Player play different formats of media files. If you encounter a media file format for which you don't have the proper codec installed, the Player will ask you if you want to download the codec. By installing all the codecs now, you'll be prepared for most files you want to play. Codecs will be discussed in greater detail in Chapter 3.

You may not need the following components:

RCA Lyra Service Provider for WMDM
You won't need this if you don't have an RCA Lyra portable device.

Adaptec CD Burning Plug-in
If you don't have a CD burner, you won't need this plug-in.

Windows Media Player skins
If you are running low on disk space, you can download skins later.

After you've decided which components to install, you're ready to move on. Click **Next**.

Deciding when to launch Windows Media Player

You will now be asked which file types you want the Player to play automatically. The dialog box looks like Figure 1.10. For more information about file associations, see Windows Help.

Figure 1.10 – *Specifying when to launch the Player.*

This dialog box is in two parts. The first part asks which file extensions you want to have associated with Windows Media Player. The second will add links to make it easy for you to launch the Player yourself.

Choosing file associations

By keeping the check boxes selected, you're telling the Player when to start up and play a file of a particular format. This ability to associate a file name extension with an application is called *file association* and is part of Windows. You'll want to leave these check boxes selected so that the Player can play all of these file types.

The file association categories are:

Additional Windows Media Formats (.wma, .wmv)
The Player already knows about .asf files, but needs to know that it can automatically play .wma and .wmv files.

MPEG Layer 3 files (.mp3, .m3u)
Keep this box selected if you want Windows Media Player to be the default player for MP3 files. These are the MP3 files that are very popular on the Internet for audio.

Other formats (.avi, .wav, .mpeg, .mpg, and more)
Keep this box selected to cover the rest of the bases. .avi, .mpg, and .mpeg are video files and .wav files are Windows audio files. The other file types include MIDI, AIFF, .ivf, and .au.

Whether you leave these file associations selected or not, you can always go back later and change them. To change file associations after the Player is installed, go to the **Tools** menu and click **Options**; then click the **Formats** tab and select the formats you want. File associations and file types will be discussed in greater detail in Chapter 3.

Adding shortcuts

You can choose whether to add a shortcut to your desktop and to the **Quick Launch** toolbar. Your choice will depend on your style of working with your programs. Selecting this option certainly makes it easy to find Windows Media Player. And if you decide that later you don't want these shortcuts, you can drag them to the Recycle Bin.

Click the **Next** button to continue.

Getting ready to install

Windows Media Player now shows you a dialog box that tells you that you're almost ready for the final installation. This gives you one last chance to cancel or to go back and change previous choices. The dialog box looks like Figure 1.11.

Figure 1.11 – *The last chance dialog box.*

You're done setting up. Click the **Next** button to finish the installation.

Installing the files

The installation program will now copy the files to their final locations, notify Windows where all the files are, and configure the Player.

You will see a dialog box like Figure 1.12. Don't click **Cancel** unless you want to stop the installation.

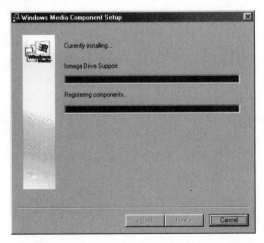

Figure 1.12 – *Watching the files fly by.*

Almost done!

There's one more thing that you need to do before you can begin enjoying music and videos on Windows Media Player. The dialog box that tells you what to do looks like Figure 1.13.

Figure 1.13 – *The last installation dialog box.*

You must restart your computer to complete the installation. If you have any other applications running at this time, be sure to close them now. Then re-start from the **Start** menu. Windows will take a few moments to restart, and you're ready to start playing.

Using auto upgrade

After you've installed Windows Media Player 7, you'll occasionally be asked if you want to find out whether newer versions of Windows Media Player ex-ist. You may want to say yes because newer versions may have exciting new features that you'll want to take advantage of.

To set the frequency at which Windows Media Player will ask you about up-grading, go to the **Tools** menu and click **Options**; then click the **Player** tab. You can choose to be asked once a day, once a week, or once a month.

You can also choose whether you want to be asked to download newer codecs when the Player encounters a file that needs a codec version it doesn't have. The default option is to ask you before downloading. If you don't want to be asked, new codecs will be downloaded automatically if you have a connection to the Internet. If you don't have an open Internet connection, the Player will ask you to connect. For more information about codecs, see Chapter 3.

Using skins

Skins provide alternate user interfaces for Windows Media Player. The Player comes with several skins, and you can create or download more. For more information about creating skins, see Part 2 of this book.

Choosing Skins

To see the skins that are currently loaded, click **Skin Chooser** in the full mode Player. It will look something like Figure 1.14.

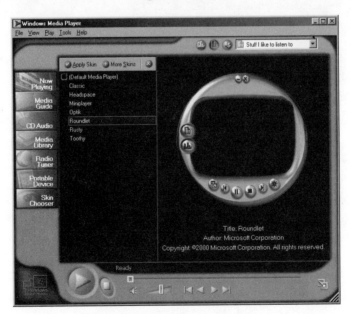

Figure 1.14 – *Skin Chooser.*

You'll see a list of installed skins. As you click on the description of each skin in the left pane, you'll see a picture of the skin in the right pane. After you've selected a skin you like, click the **Apply Skin** button to make the skin appear on your screen. The full mode of the Player will be replaced by the skin you selected.

> **Note** Not all skins support all functionality of the Player. The designer may have chosen not to implement certain options. For example, **Graphic Equalizer** sliders may not be included or a **Mute** button may not be provided.

Any time you don't like a skin, right-click it and then click the **Full Mode** option on the shortcut menu to return to full mode. Or right-click the anchor window to select a new skin.

Skins come in many different styles. For example, you can select the classic Windows Media Player skin which looks like previous versions of the Player. Figure 1.15 shows the Classic skin.

Figure 1.15 – *Windows Media Player Classic skin.*

Or you can have a skin that looks very different from a typical Windows program. Figure 1.16 shows the Cubist skin.

Figure 1.16 – *Cubist skin.*

Downloading skins

If you want to download new skins from the Internet, go to the **Skin Chooser** in the full mode Player and click the **More Skins** button. You'll be taken to the Windows Media Skin Gallery where you can find and download new skins.

You can also install a skin by double-clicking a skin file with the .wmz file extension. The Player will ask if you want to install the skin. If you say yes, it will download the skin to your computer, and start using it.

Changing modes to use the current skin

The Player has two modes: full and compact. Skins can only be displayed and used in the compact mode. The full mode view of the Player is not a skin; it provides all the functionality of Windows Media Player, while skins do not. Figure 1.17 shows the full mode view of the Player.

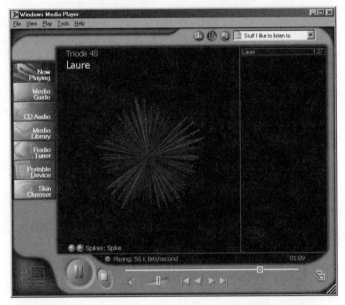

Figure 1.17 – *Full Mode Windows Media Player.*

The most recent skin you have applied is called the *current skin*. If you are in the full mode view of the Player, and you want to switch to the current skin, click the **View** menu, and then click **Compact Mode**. If you have not applied any other skins, the default skin will be applied when you click **Compact Mode**. Figure 1.18 shows the default skin. It looks much like the full mode Player but doesn't have the menus and the task bar.

Figure 1.18 – *Default skin of Windows Media Player.*

Borders

The Windows Media Player provides another type of skin called a *border*. Borders are displayed in the **Now Playing** section of the full mode Player. The purpose of borders is to include audio and video with a particular skin, creating a multimedia experience. For more information about borders, see Chapter 13.

If you apply a border and then resize the Player, some parts of the border may be cut off by the inner edges of the Player.

Using visualizations

Visualizations display synchronized animations that move in time to the music. They look similar to an oscilloscope, or to a light show where free-form images change to the rhythm and tones that are playing. You can enhance particular visualizations by choosing parameters and presets. You can learn more about visualizations and how to create them in Chapter 14.

Installing visualizations

Windows Media Player comes with several visualizations already installed. If you want to install more visualizations, connect to the Internet and then go to the **Tools** menu of the full mode Player and click the **Download Visualizations** command. You'll be taken to the Windows Media Visualizations Gallery where you can get new visualizations.

> **Note** Before you can complete the installation of a visualization, you will be asked to click Yes on a certificate such as the one in Figure 1.19.

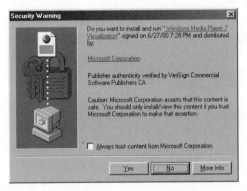

Figure 1.19 – *Digital signing dialog box for visualizations.*

The purpose of this dialog box is to identify the origin of a visualization. Visualizations must be authenticated, because they may contain small computer programs that have the potential to affect other programs or the hardware on your computer. The authentication does not mean that someone looked at and tested the visualization, it only means that you know who created the visualization.

Identifying the originator of skins is less of an issue because skins typically do not use Windows programming code, and they run inside Windows Media Player. Visualization code is written using Windows programming and runs outside of the Player, so it could cause your computer to crash if the visualization is not programmed properly.

To lessen the risk of affecting your hardware or other programs on your computer, you should only use visualizations that come from known Web sites where they have been tested and authenticated. Most visualizations you are likely to encounter on known Web sites (such as the Windows Media Visualizations Gallery) will indicate whether or not they have been tested, but as with any file that contains Windows programming code, you must be careful.

Using presets

Each visualization has one or more *presets*. Presets control the visual elements of each visualization. They can modify everything from color to pattern to speed and more. Each preset has a different name and should give you a different set of animations for a given audio stream, because it contains different values for the variables of the visualization program. You can choose the preset by clicking the **Next Preset** and **Previous Preset** buttons in the **Now Playing** pane of the full mode of Windows Media Player.

Some skins have buttons to choose presets. You can also choose specific visualizations and presets on the **View** menu by clicking the **Visualizations** command.

Using properties

In addition, some visualizations have custom properties that you can set. A property is not a fixed, predetermined group of settings like a preset, but gives you a set of specific options that you can choose from. For example, you can choose from a list of colors, set the speed exactly, or select a picture from a menu. To set the custom properties of a visualization, go to the **Tools** menu and click **Options**; then click the **Visualizations** tab.

Using full-screen visualizations

Some visualizations can be displayed in full-screen mode, filling up the entire computer display area and not just the Player window. Press the ALT and ENTER keys simultaneously to make your visualizations occupy the entire screen of your computer. You can also select **Full Screen** from the **View** menu of the full mode Player or from the shortcut menu of a compact mode Player. To return from full-screen mode, press ALT and ENTER again.

You may need a fast computer for some visualizations to work well in full-screen mode.

CHAPTER 2

How Does the Player Work?

In this chapter you'll learn how to operate Windows Media Player 7. You'll see how to play files, use the buttons to navigate, change the settings, use the menus, and switch to different views and modes. You'll also be shown how to find files on the Internet, copy music from CDs, and use playlists.

Playing a file in only three steps

Playing music or video on the Player is a simple 1-2-3 process:

1. Go to the **Now Playing** view.

2. Pick a song from a playlist and click the song title.

3. Then click the **Play** button to begin playing.

The three steps to playing a song are shown below in more detail.

Step 1: Start with the full mode Player

When you start Windows Media Player 7 for the first time, and you are connected to the Internet, you should see the full mode Player in the **Media Guide** view. Figure 2.1a shows a typical **Media Guide** view.

Figure 2.1a - *Full mode Player in **Media Guide** view with Internet connection.*

The **Media Guide** is a Web site that gives you a doorway into the world of audio and video on the Internet. The contents change nearly every day, giving you new audio and video selections, current entertainment news, and free downloads.

If you are *not* connected to the Internet, you'll see a screen similar to Figure 2.1b.

Figure 2.1b – *Media Guide view without an Internet connection.*

You can now get started using Windows Media Player. Click **Now Playing** on the left side of the full mode Player. You should see a view similar to Figure 2.2.

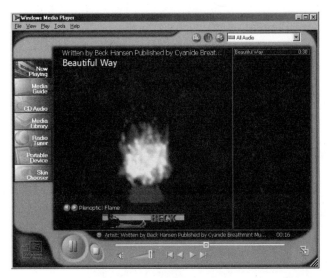

Figure 2.2 – *Windows Media Player in full mode in the **Now Playing** view.*

If you don't see something like Figure 2.2, you're probably looking at a skin. A skin may have been loaded by the last person to use the Player; you won't be able to see the **Now Playing** view when a skin is running. If you are viewing a skin, you will want to return to the full mode of Windows Media Player.

Windows Media Player comes in two modes: full mode and compact mode. The compact mode is used to display skins, and the full mode displays the standard Player. To return to full mode from any skin, right-click anywhere on the skin and then click **Return to Full Mode** on the shortcut menu that appears.

The full mode has several different views it can display. Right now, all you want to do is play a file, so click **Now Playing** at the left side of the full mode Player. You should now see something that looks close to Figure 2.2. You probably will have a different visualization or a different playlist loaded on your computer, but you're ready to start.

Step 2: Choose a song

There are several ways to choose a file to play, but the easiest way is to use a playlist. Playlists will be covered in greater detail later in this chapter, but to get you started, use the playlist that should be visible on the right side of the **Now Playing** view.

Figure 2.3 shows a **Now Playing** view with a playlist named "All Audio" that contains all the songs that the Player has information about. The third song, "Laure", is selected and playing. You can double-click any item in the playlist to start playing that item.

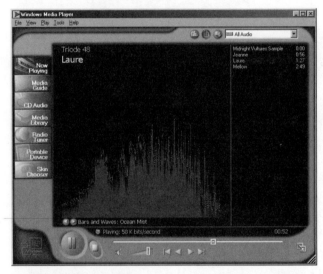

Figure 2.3 – *A playlist with more than one item.*

You can learn more about using playlists later in this chapter. There are other ways to choose audio and video files as well, and they will also be covered in this chapter.

Step 3: Click Play

Now that you've selected a song title, click the **Play** button. It looks like an arrow that is pointing to the right. You can see it in Figure 2.4.

Figure 2.4 – *The **Play** button of the full mode Player.*

When you click the **Play** button, two things happen. The music starts playing and the button changes. The button now looks like Figure 2.5.

Figure 2.5 – *The **Pause** button of the full mode Player.*

This new button is the **Pause** button. Any time you want to stop the Player, just click the **Pause** button. That will stop the music playing and change the **Pause** button back to a **Play** button.

Using the navigation buttons

Windows Media Player has several other buttons you can use to enhance your playing experience. The following buttons are always at the bottom of the window in the full mode Player and are listed here from left to right:

- **Play/Pause**
- **Stop**
- **Seek**
- **Mute**
- **Volume**
- **Previous**
- **Fast Reverse**
- **Fast Forward**
- **Next**
- **Switch to compact mode**

If you hover over a button with the mouse pointer, the name of the button will appear.

Figure 2.6 shows the navigation buttons for the full mode Player. These buttons are also called transport buttons and use symbols that are common to the electronic industry for controlling tape recorders, VCRs, and CD players. You'll often see the same button symbols in skins, but because every artist designs skins his own way, and the artwork varies widely, you won't necessarily find all the same buttons in each skin, or the buttons may not be in the same order.

Figure 2.6 – *Navigation buttons.*

Here is a brief explanation of each button.

Play/Pause

This button toggles back and forth between two states: **Play** and **Pause**. **Play** starts the selected music or video playing, and **Pause** pauses it. Clicking **Play** from a paused state will start the program playing from the same position it was paused at.

Stop

This button stops a currently playing program. If you click **Play** after clicking **Stop**, the program will start over at the beginning.

Seek

This is the long bar that extends above the other buttons. The **Seek** bar shows the current position in the file. If you click and drag the tiny box, you can change the current position in the file to anywhere you want. The left end of the **Seek** bar represents the beginning of the file, and the right end represents the end of the file. So the midpoint of the bar represents the midpoint of the file, regardless of its length.

Mute

Click this to mute the sound of the currently playing file. Click it again to return the sound to its previous volume.

Volume

This is a short triangular bar with a box above it. Click and drag the box left or right to increase or decrease the volume of the sound.

Previous

Click this to go to the previous title in a playlist.

Fast Reverse

Click this to move the current seek position of the file backward. Click it again to start playing from the new seek position. This button only works for video files that use the Windows Media video file format.

Fast Forward

Click this to move the current seek position of the file forward. Click it again to start playing from the new seek position. This button only works for video files that use the Windows Media video file format.

Next

Click this to go to the next title in the playlist.

Switch to compact mode

Use this to change the Player display to compact mode. This will change the user interface to the default skin or the last skin you selected.

Watching visualizations

At the bottom of the left side of the **Now Playing** pane, you'll see two buttons. Click these to change visualization presets. These buttons are shown in Figure 2.7.

Figure 2.7 – *Previous visualization and Next visualization preset buttons.*

Visualizations draw moving shapes and colors on the screen that rise and fall in time to the beat and tone of the music. Several visualizations are included with Windows Media Player, and more are available from the Windows Media Player Visualizations Gallery. Click **Download Visualizations** on the **Tools** menu to go there.

Each visualization has several presets. Each preset gives a different "flavor" or "twist" to the visualization; for example, one preset might make all the colors soft pastels and another preset would make them vivid primary colors. You can change visualizations and presets by clicking the **Previous visualization** and **Next visualization** buttons. The visualization and preset names are displayed to the right of the buttons, with the visualization name first, and the preset name following, separated by a colon.

You won't see a visualization if you're playing a video, because they both use the same display pane.

Changing other settings

There's one other button that can be useful when playing audio and video. At the top of the full mode Windows Media Player, just to the right of center, you'll see the **Show Equalizer & Settings** button that looks like Figure 2.8.

Figure 2.8 – *Show/Hide Equalizer & Settings in Now Playing button.*

Clicking this button will show a new pane in the **Now Playing** area that is below the visualization/video pane. This pane covers several settings. To move to a new setting, click the **Previous setting** or **Next setting** button. These buttons are shown in Figure 2.9.

Figure 2.9 – *Previous setting and Next setting buttons.*

The following settings are accessed from this pane by clicking the **Previous setting** and **Next setting** buttons:

- **SRS WOW Effects**
- **Graphic Equalizer**
- **Video Settings**
- **Windows Media Information**
- **Captions**

Here is a brief explanation of each setting.

SRS WOW Effects settings

This pane allows you to adjust the SRS WOW settings. SRS is a type of surround sound that makes your audio sound more lifelike and three-dimensional. You can see the **SRS WOW Effects** pane in Figure 2.10.

Figure 2.10 – *SRS WOW Effects pane.*

On the right is the logo for SRS. Click it to find out more about SRS. On the left are two horizontal sliders that adjust the **TruBass** and **WOW Effect**. Between the two sliders and the SRS logo are two buttons: the top turns SRS on and off, and the bottom one toggles between various presets.

Here is a brief explanation of each button:

TruBass
> Sliding this all the way to the right increases the bass enhancement of the audio. Sliding to the left decreases it.

WOW Effect
> Sliding this to the right increases the perceived height and width of the audio image.

On/Off
> Click this toggle button to turn the **SRS WOW Effects** on or off.

Speaker Settings
> Click this to toggle through the following speaker settings: normal speakers, large speakers, and headphones.

Graphic Equalizer settings

This pane allows you to adjust the audio to make it sound exactly the way you'd like. If you want to boost the bass or cut out high notes, this is the place to do it. Figure 2.11 shows the **Graphic Equalizer** pane.

Figure 2.11 – *Graphic Equalizer pane.*

On the left you see ten sliders that correspond to ten divisions of the audio spectrum. Move the leftmost slider up to increase the power of the lowest frequencies, move it down to reduce them. Similarly, the rightmost slider controls the upper tenth of the spectrum (the highest frequencies). Play with the sliders to see what sounds good to you.

To the immediate right of the sliders are two buttons. The top one turns the graphic equalizer on or off. If it is off, the settings are completely "flat," that is, no modification is made to the sounds. The bottom button toggles through several presets that are based on popular styles of music. For example, the **Jazz** preset will boost the middle frequencies more than the **Acoustic** setting. If you make changes in the **Custom** preset, those changes will be saved for the next time you use the Player.

To the right of those two buttons is a final horizontal slider that allows you to adjust the stereo balance. Move it to the left to increase the apparent volume of the left channel and to the right to increase the right volume.

Video settings

This pane allows you to adjust the video to make it look the way you like it. If you want to adjust the brightness or the intensity of the color, this is the place to do it. Figure 2.12 shows the **Video Settings** pane.

Figure 2.12 – *Video Settings pane.*

On the left side of the pane are four horizontal sliders. They adjust the **Brightness**, **Contrast**, **Hue**, and **Saturation** of the video picture. To the right of these sliders is a button that resets all the sliders to their default (centered) positions.

Here is a brief explanation of each slider:

Brightness

This adjusts the brightness of the video picture. Slide it all the way to the left to make the picture completely black and all the way to the right to make it completely white. Usually you'll want it somewhere in between.

Contrast

Use this to sharpen or blur video images. Moving this slider all the way to the left makes the picture sharper. This effect is sometimes known as posterization. Moving it to the right makes the image look blurry, as if everything was photographed in a dense fog or underwater.

Hue

Adjust the hue for basic color changes. Slide it to the left to make everything more red/purple and to the right for green.

Saturation

This adjusts how much color is shown in the video. Slide the slider all the way to the left, and only the gray tones are used, with no color at all. Slide it all the way to the right, and the colors are extremely intense (saturated).

Windows Media Information

This pane isn't really a setting, but shows additional information about a particular item. For example, if you load the **Sample Playlist**, and open the **Windows Media Information** pane, you'll see something like Figure 2.13.

Figure 2.13 – *Windows Media Information pane.*

The **Windows Media Information** pane can display details such as genre and label, but can also display pictures, links, and other useful information. In this example, if you click the album cover or the link to the right of it, you'll be taken to a Web page that gives more details about the artist, album, label, and so on. For more information on how to create advertising information such as the kind you see in the **Windows Media Information** pane, see Chapter 13.

Captions

This pane isn't really a setting either, but shows captions for video files. See Figure 2.14 for a typical caption file.

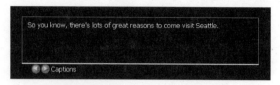

Figure 2.14 – *Captions* *pane.*

For more information about captions, see Chapter 13.

Using menus

Many of the operations you can perform with buttons can also be done through menus. The **File** menu is always available in the full mode view but is also available in skins that provide menus. Here is a brief listing of each menu item and what it does.

File menu

The **File** menu helps you work with files. The following commands are available on the **File** menu:

Open
Use this to load a file, using the standard Windows **Open** dialog box. The file you select will be loaded into a new playlist, and the file will start playing.

Open URL
Use this to load a file from a Web site or over a network. A URL (Uniform Resource Locator) is a path to a file; for example, *http:// internalsite/laure.wma* is a URL. You must type a URL that links to an audio or video file. If you type a URL to a Web page, you will get an error.

Close
This doesn't close the Player; it closes the media file that is playing. It stops the Player and deselects the current item in the current playlist.

Add to Library

Use this to add a track to the media library. The media library is the collection of all audio and video that the Player has information about. When you select this option, you are given three choices: **Add Currently Playing Track**, **Add File**, and **Add URL**. The first choice is useful when you want to add the content that is currently playing to the media library. The second and third choices are similar to the **Open** and **Open URL** commands on the **File** menu except that instead of playing the file, the Player just adds it to the media library.

Import Playlist to Library

Use this to import a playlist into the media library. Playlists are Windows Media metafiles that have an extension of .asx, .wax, .wvx. You can also import a .m3u file which will automatically be converted to a playlist.

Export Playlist to File

Use this to save a selected playlist in a text file. If you don't have any playlists selected (or any playlists at all), the media library will be saved as a playlist.

Copy to CD

Use this to copy files to a CD. You must have a CD-ROM that is recordable and a CD drive capable of recording. For more information about copying files to a CD-ROM, see Chapter 3. You may not see this menu item if you do not have a recordable CD drive installed on your computer.

Properties

Selecting this will display information about the audio or video that is currently playing.

Work Offline

Use this option if you don't want the Player to go out to the Internet to gather information about CDs.

Exit

This will shut down Windows Media Player.

View menu

The **View** menu helps you see all the different parts of Windows Media Player and work with visual elements. The following commands are available through the **View** menu:

Full Mode

This option returns you to the full mode view.

Compact Mode

Use this to change from full mode to a skin. Whatever skin you used last will be the default skin.

Now Playing Tools

Select this to change how the **Now Playing** area looks. You can choose to hide or display the playlist, title, and visualization portions of the pane. You can also show or hide the following settings: **SRS WOW Effects**, **Graphic Equalizer**, **Video**, **Windows Media Information**, and **Captions**. Finally, you can also hide or show the resize bars, which are the bars that separate the sub-panes of the **Now Playing** area.

Task Bar

The **Task Bar** menu command provides access to the same features found on the **Task Bar** tabs at the left side of the full mode Player. The following features are provided: **Now Playing**, **Media Guide**, **CD Audio**, **Media Library**, **Radio Tuner**, **Portable Device**, and **Skin Chooser**. For more information about the **Task Bar**, see the "Changing views in full mode" section of this chapter.

Visualizations

Selecting this option provides a list of the currently loaded visualizations. Selecting a visualization shows you the presets that are available for each visualization.

File Markers

Use this to go to a specific position in a file that has markers. If a file doesn't have markers, you can't select this option. For more information about file markers, see Chapter 12.

Statistics

Selecting this option can show you how well the file is playing. This can be particularly useful if you want to report problems with files that you are receiving in real time through the Internet (called streaming). If there are problems, you usually will know, but this option can give you exact answers, such as how many packets are being lost during transmission.

Full Screen

If you are playing a visualization that supports it, use this option to have the visualization display over the full screen of your computer. Once in full screen, you can return to normal mode by pressing the ALT and ENTER keys simultaneously.

Refresh

Use this to refresh the page when you are using the **Media Guide**, **Portable Device**, or **Radio Tuner** panes. If you think you're looking at yesterday's Web page, you may be right. Some information in these task panes is cached, that is, stored on your hard disk, depending on the settings in Internet Explorer or your portable device.

Zoom

This allows you to change the size of a video that is playing. You can choose to make it fit the screen, or pick a specific percentage of the original. The percentages are 50%, 100%, and 200%.

Play menu

The **Play** menu gives you most of the same options that the transport buttons offer. The following commands are available through the **Play** menu:

Play/Pause

This starts the music or video program playing, or if it is already playing, pauses it. The Player must have at least one item in the media library in order to play. Playing a paused file starts the file playing at the same position it was paused at.

Stop

This stops the currently playing program. If you click **Play** after stopping the program, the song or video will start over at the beginning.

Skip Back

This stops the currently playing item in the playlist and plays the previous item in the same playlist. This corresponds to the **Previous** button in the Player buttons at the bottom of the full mode Player. If you are at the first item in a playlist and you select **Skip Back**, the last item in the playlist will be played.

Skip Forward

This stops the currently playing item in the playlist and plays the next item in the same playlist. This corresponds to the **Next** button in the Player buttons at the bottom of the full mode Player. If you are at the last item in a playlist and you select **Skip Forward**, the first item in the playlist will be played.

Rewind

This rewinds a video in short intervals. You can only rewind videos that are encoded in Windows Media Format. This corresponds to the **Fast Reverse** button in the Player buttons at the bottom of the full mode Player.

Fast Forward

This fast forwards a video in short intervals. You can only fast forward videos that are encoded in Windows Media Format. This corresponds to the **Fast Forward** button in the Player buttons at the bottom of the full mode Player.

Shuffle

This plays the items in the current playlist in a random order. It does not change the order of the items in the playlist, only the order in which they are played while the shuffle option is selected.

Repeat

This repeats the playing of the entire current playlist, not specific items in a playlist. If you want to repeat only one item, create a new playlist, put only that item in it, and repeat that playlist.

Volume

This lets you nudge the volume up or down by a small amount. It also allows you to mute the volume.

Tools menu

The **Tools** menu is for advanced features of Windows Media Player. The following commands are available through the **Tools** menu:

Download Visualizations

Select this to go to a Web page that will let you download new visualizations.

Search Computer for Media

Use this to search your computer for all audio and video files. The Player will add the files it finds to your media library and divide them between the audio and video collections. If you choose the option to search for WAV and MIDI files, you will add a lot of Windows sound effects that you may not want to play with the Player; on the other hand, you may discover some interesting MIDI files that are hidden away inside your Windows folder. You can choose to load from local drives, network drives, all drives, or a specific drive, and even a specific directory. If you have mapped a network drive to your computer, you can search that drive as well. For example, if drive X: is mapped to a network drive, you can search that drive, or directories on that drive.

License Management

If you download music that requires a license, or make copies of CD tracks, this option specifies where you want to store the licenses on your computer. You might want to pick a folder that you can find easily so you can conveniently back up your licenses to another drive or storage medium. If you pay for a song and the song needs a license to play, you'll want to take good care of your licenses. For more information about licensing, see "Understanding digital rights" in Chapter 3.

Options

This is the option for everything else not covered in other menu items. The following section, "Options dialog box," provides more information about this menu item.

Options dialog box

If you go to the **Tools** menu and click **Options**, the **Options** dialog box is displayed. It covers various options you may want to change. The following tabs are included in the **Options** dialog box:

Player

This tab lets you set how often you want Windows Media Player to check for software upgrades (daily, weekly, monthly), whether you want the Player to automatically download codecs it needs (See Chapter 3 for more about codecs.), whether you want the Player to identify itself to Web sites and download licenses automatically, whether you want the Player to start up in **Media Guide** (instead of whatever you mode you used last time), and whether you want skins to be on top of other windows. You can also decide whether you want the anchor to be displayed when using skins. The anchor window is a small window that appears in the lower right corner of the screen when Windows Media Player is in compact mode. You can click the anchor window, and then click **Return to Full Mode** to return to the full mode of the Player. Most of the time you'll want to leave these options the way they were initially set.

Network

If you are an advanced networking user, you can use this tab to set proxies, ports, and protocols.

CD Audio

Use this to set up how you will play or record CDs. For playing CDs, you can choose whether to use digital playback, if your computer supports it, and whether to use error correction. Change these options if you are having problems playing CDs. For copying music from CDs, you can select how much compression to use when converting music from CD format to music file formats. You'll have to choose between smaller file sizes and better quality. You can also choose whether to use digital copying or error correction, and whether to use personal rights management. Finally, you can choose what folder you want the copied audio files to be created in. For more information about copying CDs and digital rights, see Chapter 3.

Portable Device

If you have a portable device, you can use this pane to decide whether to let the Player convert the music automatically or let you pick a tradeoff between file size and audio quality. You can also click a button and find out what devices are supported by Windows Media Player. For more information about portable devices, see Chapter 5.

Performance

You might want to use this tab if you are having trouble with viewing live files (streaming). You can tell the Player what network connection you have, how much buffering to do, whether you want to use hardware acceleration with video, and how to adjust digital video settings. For more information about streaming, see Chapter 4.

Media Library

Use this tab to set access rights to your media library. You can specify what levels of access you want to grant outside Web sites to read or modify the media in your library. This involves both security and privacy issues. This also specifies whether you want Internet music purchases to be added to your library automatically.

Visualizations

If you have installed a visualization that has properties you can change, go to this tab to change them. For example, the Ambience visualization will let you set the full-screen size and offscreen buffer size. You can also use this tab to load a visualization that is stored on your computer but that is not registered with the Player. Be sure you know the source of any visualization before loading, and load them from only trusted sites, so that you can avoid viruses.

Formats

Use this tab to make sure the Player plays the file formats you want it to play. If another brand of player starts playing a file that you want Windows Media Player to play, change the file association here, if it is a file format the Player can play.

Help menu

The **Help** menu gives you help and information. This menu has the following three commands:

Help Topics

This command launches the Help file that comes with Windows Media Player. The Help file covers all the features you need to know about to use the Player. You can also get the Help file by pressing the F1 key on your computer at any time while Window Media Player is the active Window.

Check For Player Upgrades

Use this command any time you're curious about upgrades to Windows Media Player. The Player will do this automatically for you, but you may want to do it yourself if you've heard news of a new version.

About Windows Media Player

This will display the name, copyright, version number, and product ID of Windows Media Player.

Compact mode shortcut menu

When Windows Media Player is in compact mode, you can right-click the skin and get a menu. Each of the commands on the menu corresponds to a similarly named command on one of the menus of the full mode Player.

Table 2.1 shows the commands on the menu of the compact mode along with their corresponding full mode menu commands.

Compact mode menu command	Full mode menu command
Open	**File** menu **Open** option
Open URL	**File** menu **Open URL** option
Shuffle	**Play** menu **Shuffle** option
Repeat	**Play** menu **Repeat** option
Volume	**Play** menu **Volume** option
Play/Pause	**Play** menu **Play/Pause** option
Stop	**Play** menu **Stop** option
Skip Back	**Play** menu **Skip Back** option
Skip Forward	**Play** menu **Skip Back** option
Return to Full Mode	**Play** menu **Skip Forward** option
Full Screen	**View** menu **Full Screen** option
Properties	**File** menu **Properties** option
Statistics	**View** menu **Statistics** option
Options	**Tools** menu **Options** option
Help	**Help** menu **Help Topics** option
About	**Help** menu **About Windows Media Player** option
Exit	**File** menu **Exit** option

Table 2.1 – *Menu commands of the compact mode Player.*

Changing views in full mode

The full mode of Windows Media Player has seven views that are accessed by clicking tabs on the **Task Bar**, which is on the left side of the window. Each view gives you a different way to interact with audio and video. Here is a list of the views:

Now Playing

This view shows a visualization or video on the left pane and a playlist on the right. You can also display a hidden settings pane to make various adjustments or see additional information. You'll spend most of your time in this view.

Media Guide

This is the default view of the Player and opens up a world of audio and video through the Internet. You can get daily news of new audio and video releases, tune in to Internet radio stations, and download tons of things to see and hear, most of it free! For more help with downloading, see the "Finding files on the Internet" section in this chapter.

CD Audio

If you have a CD player in your computer, you can play your CD tracks using Windows Media Player. For more information about using CDs, see the "Copying music from CDs" section in this chapter. For more information about creating your own CDs, see Chapter 3.

Media Library

This is where you can organize all your audio and video. You can search for audio and video files on your computer, create playlists, and change your Internet radio presets here. For more information about working with playlists, see the "Using playlists" section of this chapter.

Radio Tuner

Use this feature to search out and sort Internet radio stations. From around the world or around the block, you can listen to music every hour of every day and never hear the same thing twice!

Portable Devices

Use this pane to download music to your Pocket PC or other portable device. For more information about portable devices, see Chapter 5.

Skin Chooser

Use this to apply skins that came with your installation. You can also use this feature to download new skins from the Windows Media Skins Gallery Web site. Once you try one skin, you'll never want to stop! New skins will be appearing frequently, so check this site often.

Finding files on the Internet

Now that you know how to use the Windows Media Player, you can go out on the Web and find more music. You can use a browser to do this of course, but Windows Media Player gives you a special window to the world of music and video. This window is called the **Media Guide**. Earlier in this chapter you saw a typical view of the **Media Guide** in Figure 2.1a.

The Player will start up with the **Media Guide** view. You can always get to it by using the full mode of the Player and clicking **Media Guide** on the **Task Bar** on the left side of the Player. If you don't want **Media Guide** to be the default view, go to the **Tools** menu and click **Options**; then click the **Player** tab and clear the **Start Player in Media Guide** check box.

The **Media Guide** is a window to the WindowsMedia.com Web site. The **Media Guide** has hundreds of links to new audio and video files to play and download, and gives you lots of information about what's new in the world of audio and video. You can spend hours and hours exploring the **Media Guide**.

For more information about file formats you can download, see Chapter 3. For information about seeing and hearing files without waiting to download them (streaming), see Chapter 4.

Copying music from CDs

If you want to listen to music from different CDs without inserting and removing your CDs all the time, Windows Media Player can save you a lot of time. All you have to do is copy the CD (or just the tracks you want) onto your computer, then assemble the tracks into playlists and create your own customized musical experience.

Also, you can have the Player compress the files so they won't take up as much room on your hard disk. You can control the amount of compression you need. Choosing high compression will create files that won't sound as good but will take up less space.

Copying tracks

Copying CD tracks is extremely easy. All you need to do is load a CD into your CD-ROM drive and start Windows Media Player. When the Player starts, it loads the CD tracks into a playlist and displays the **CD Audio** pane of the full mode Player. Figure 2.15 shows a typical **CD Audio** pane, which you can always get to from the full mode view of the Player by clicking the **CD Audio** tab of the **Task Bar** on the left side of the Player.

If you are connected to the Internet, the Player will go out to a database and get information about each track on the CD, showing you not only track names and lengths, but artist, genre, style, and so on. On many CDs, you can even click the **Album Details** and go to a Web site that contains more information about the CD.

After you've loaded your CD, all you have to do is decide which tracks you want to copy to your computer. After you've decided, select the check box at the left of each track to select the tracks you want to copy.

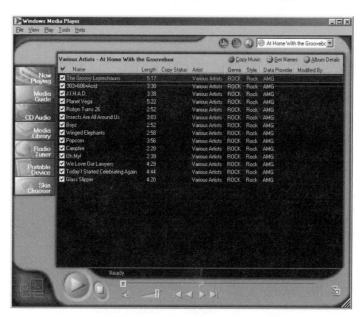

Figure 2.15 – *Audio CD pane.*

When you're ready to copy, just click the red **Copy Music** button. You'll see that the Player starts copying because there is a Copy Status column in the

CD Audio playlist, and the status will be displayed. Files that are being copied will have a percent-copied display; files that will be copied are labeled "Pending" and when a file is finished copying, it will be labeled "Copied to Library" in the status column.

Selecting copy options

There are several options you can select that will allow you to change the way that the Player copies files from a CD to your computer. Click **Options** on the **Tools** menu, and then click the **CD Audio** tab. You'll see the following choices:

Digital playback (under Playback Settings)
> This setting only applies to playback, not to copying CDs. If your computer supports digital playback, select this check box and see how digital playback sounds. If you don't select this option, you will not be able to see visualizations.

Use error correction (under Playback Settings)
> This setting only applies to playback, not to copying CDs. If you are experiencing a lot of errors, selecting this check box may help correct them during playback. You'll know you're getting errors if the audio sounds as if parts are missing or the video starts jumping around and missing frames. You can only select this if you have also selected the **Digital playback** check box.

Copy music at this quality (under Copying Settings)
> Windows Media Player can compress the digital information in the files it creates so that the files will be smaller. It does this using a variety of techniques. Depending on the type of music you're copying, you may or may not notice the difference. You can choose the amount of compression with a slider bar. An average music CD can be compressed from as small as 28 MB to as large as 70 MB. The larger the file, the better the sound quality.

Digital copying (under Copying Settings)
> Select this check box to copy CD tracks to audio files that enable digital playback. Not all computers and sound cards have digital playback. If yours do, this is a good option to use, and the sound doesn't need to be converted to analog and back to digital. If you're not sure, try a track both ways and see what you like.

Use error correction (under Copying Settings)

You can only select this check box if you've also selected the **Digital copying** option. Use this if your tracks are producing errors. Once again, if you're not sure whether to use this, try a track both ways and listen to the results.

Enable Personal Rights Management (under Copying Settings)

If this check box is selected, the files you create will have information attached to them indicating that they were created on your computer. You will definitely want to keep this option checked if you want to copy your files to a portable device such as a Pocket PC; many portable devices will not play music if you have not licensed the appropriate rights for a particular file. However, if you keep this option checked, you cannot play files you have copied on another computer. So if you want to copy files from your CD and then transfer them to another computer, you should not select this option. Of course, before copying and transferring, be sure you have the legal right to do so. The issues of digital rights are covered in Chapter 3.

Using playlists

A playlist is a convenient way to organize groups of audio and video files. The term comes from the radio industry and refers to the list of songs that a disc jockey plays on a particular radio program.

You might want to make up playlists for different performers or different kinds of music or videos. You can shuffle playlists or repeat them endlessly. This way, you can create a media experience that is continuously entertaining.

You can see which playlist is playing by looking in the upper-right corner of the full mode Player. You will see a drop-down list box, which shows the current playlist.

Using the Media Library

The **Media Library** is the key to understanding playlists. The **Media Library** is where you create your playlists. You can get to the **Media Library** by choosing the **Media Library** tab on the **Task Bar** of the full mode Windows Media Player. Figure 2.16 shows a typical view of the **Media Library**.

Figure 2.16 – *Media Library*.

On the left side of the **Media Library** you'll see a tree-like list of all the audio and video that the Player has information about, as well as all playlists and radio presets. This is set up similar to Microsoft Windows Explorer in that you click an item on the left and the contents of that item appear on the right.

The **Media Library** is divided into the following sections:

- Audio
- Video
- My Playlists
- Radio Tuner Presets
- Deleted Items

Each section is a node in the tree. Figure 2.17 shows the five nodes of the **Media Library**.

Figure 2.17 – *Five nodes of the **Media Library***.

Figure 2.18 shows the nodes expanded by one level for each node. You can expand a node to show the items inside it by clicking the plus sign to the left of the node name.

Figure 2.18 – ***Media Library** nodes expanded by one level*.

You can explore the contents of the **Media Library** by expanding the nodes. Any time you click one of the node item names, the contents of that node, if it is a folder, will be displayed in the right pane of the **Media Library**.

Understanding the audio collection

The audio collection is the part of the library that keeps track of audio files on your computer and other audio files that the Player has information about (for example, files on the Internet).

Adding Audio Files

You can add to the audio collection in several ways:

- Click the **File** menu, click **Open**, and then choose an audio file.

- Click the **File** menu, click **Open URL**, and then choose an audio file.

- Click the **File** menu, click **Add to Library**, and then choose an audio file.

- Click the **File** menu, and click **Import Playlist to Library** (if the playlist has links to audio files in it).

- From the **CD Audio** task pane, copy a CD track to your computer.

- Start an audio file playing by double-clicking it.

- Start an audio file playing by right-clicking it and selecting the **Play** option.

Sorting audio files

You can find a file by clicking the **Search** button at the top of the **Media Library** pane.

The Audio collection is a database of audio files, and like other databases, it stores not only the file name and location of audio files, but additional information such as artist, album, and genre. This additional information is used to sort the Audio collection into at least four categories. You can see the categories by clicking the nodes to the left of the **Audio** label. Figure 2.19 shows the four nodes inside the Audio collection.

Figure 2.19 – *The four nodes of the audio collection.*

Here is an explanation of each category:

All Audio
> This includes a list of all audio that Windows Media Player has information about.

Album
> This shows a list of all music that is associated with albums. The album information can come from a CD, from a playlist, or can be embedded in the file itself. The Player can get album information about CDs from Internet databases.

Artist

You can see a list of all the artists that are associated with the audio files in the Audio collection.

Genre

If you want to find audio files that have a genre associated with them, this is the place to look.

Understanding the video collection

The video collection uses the same concepts as the audio collection except that it keeps track of video files. Instead of **All Audio**, the video collection will refer to **All Clips**, **Artist** becomes **Author**, and there is no album or genre equivalent for videos.

Understanding My Playlists

This is a collection of all playlists that the Player has information about. Playlists are lists that you create of audio and video content.

Creating playlists

Creating playlists couldn't be simpler. Click the **New Playlist** button at the top left of the **Media Library** and enter the new playlist name.

Adding to playlists

You can add to playlists by doing the following:

1. Create your playlist.

2. Find the audio or video file you want to add. You must open an Audio or Video collection and select a file from the collection. For example, open the Audio collection, then open the Artist collection, choose an artist you like, displaying all the songs by that artist in the right pane.

3. Select the audio or video file, and add it to the playlist. You can do this in one of two ways. The easy way is to right-click the file and choose the **Add to Playlist** option. You'll be provided with a list of playlists. Pick one and you're done. There's also an **Add to Playlist** button at the top of the **Media Library** pane if you prefer to click a button.

4. You can also select the audio or video file and drag it to the playlist in the left pane. This requires a bit of opening and closing of nodes in the collection, but after you get used to it, you'll find that this is a useful way to work with complicated playlists.

Deleting and renaming playlists

You can also delete and rename playlists by right-clicking a playlist and choosing the delete or rename option. Deleted playlists aren't really deleted, they are transferred to the **Deleted Items** part of the **Media Library**.

Deleting media items and playlists

If you delete an item in the audio or video collection, the item is transferred to the **Deleted Items** part of the **Media Library**. The same is true for deleted playlists. This is similar to the Recycle Bin in Windows.

Restoring media items and playlists

You can get the file or playlist back by right-clicking it and selecting the **Restore** option. The file or playlist will return to the place you deleted it from.

Permanently deleting media items and playlists

If you want to permanently erase the media items and playlists you deleted, you can reclaim their disk space by right-clicking the **Deleted Items** node and choosing the **Empty Deleted Items** option. Be careful! After you do this, you can't go back! But at least you're given an option to change your mind before the media files and playlists are gone forever.

Using the Radio Tuner

The **Radio Tuner** feature lets you use the Player to listen to Internet radio stations from around the world. Thousands of stations broadcast audio programs of music, news, and commentary.

Figure 2.20 shows the **Radio Tuner** view, which you can get to by clicking **Radio Tuner** in the task bar on the left side of the full mode of Windows Media Player.

Figure 2.20 – *Radio Tuner view in the full mode Player.*

The **Radio Tuner** view has two panes: Station Finder and Presets.

Using Station Finder

The **Station Finder** can help you tune in to Internet Radio stations. Even though there are thousands of stations around the globe, you can easily find one you like with only a few clicks. The contents of the **Station Finder** are updated frequently by WindowsMedia.com so that as new stations go on the air, you can tune in to them right away.

All the stations are listed in a table that sorts them by station name, speed, frequency, and format or city. You can sort the table rows by clicking the column heading you want to sort on. Double-click a station listing to start it playing.

Above the table of radio stations is one or more list boxes. The box on the left has several categories that you can use to find particular radio stations, including the following:

Format
This gives you a set of predefined radio station formats ranging from Alternative Rock to Classical to News Radio.

Band

You can choose to search through the AM band or FM band, or choose Internet-only.

Language

There are several spoken languages to choose from, including Chinese, English, Latvian, and 20 others.

Location

Countries such as the United States, Finland, Korea, and 30 others are represented in the table listings with radio stations. If you choose the United States, you can search by state.

Callsign

If you know the call letters of a radio station, you can find the station by typing the call letters in the search box. For example, if you type "CKWW", you'll listen to station CKWW in Detroit, Michigan, that specializes in big band music.

Frequency

You can tune in to a station by typing the frequency; for example, 88.5 on the FM dial would give you radio station KPLU in the Seattle, Washington, area.

Keyword

If a station has a slogan, you can find it with a keyword. For example, searching for "oldies" will give you several stations to choose from.

Using station presets

There are two default presets that you can use to sort radio stations that you will want to use often. One is called Featured and has stations that are currently featured by Windows Media Player. You can't add stations to Featured. But you can add radio stations that you want to use frequently to My Presets.

You can create your own preset categories by clicking the **Edit** button above the **Presets** list.

Working with radio stations in the Media Library

All presets created in the **Radio Tuner** are automatically copied to the **Media Library** in the **Radio Tuner Presets** category.

CHAPTER 3

Understanding Media Files

This chapter covers the concepts of computer files that relate to Windows Media Player. It will explain what types of files the Player plays, how the licensing of files addresses digital rights, and how you can copy files to a CD with the **CD Audio** feature.

Audio and video are stored on computers in files. Because a great deal of digital information is needed to store every minute of media on a computer, files must be compressed to ease storage space and shorten the time it takes to copy a file over a network. Files can be compressed in many different ways. The mathematical formula that is used to compress and decode a file is called a *codec*. This chapter covers the many different types of file formats and codecs that Windows Media Player uses.

Information about the ownership of audio or video content can also be stored in a file. Digital rights management (DRM) is one of the new features that Windows Media Player provides to give media copyright owners the ability to control who can play a file. You can read about digital rights in this chapter and learn how the Player can make it easier to use files that are secured with DRM.

You can create your own files on a music CD using the new **CD Audio** feature of Windows Media Player. Assuming you have a CD recorder in your computer, you can copy music from your hard disk to a blank recordable CD in only a few minutes. Copying audio to a new CD is called *burning*. This chapter will show you how to prepare your files and burn them to a CD.

File formats

Computers store digital data in files. An audio file consists of an array of numbers. Each number represents the volume and frequency of sound at one instant of time. Put all the numbers together and you have a changing stream of sound frequencies and volumes that will be speech, music, or sound effects. Video files are similar but use numbers to define the color and brightness of each part of the quickly changing set of frames that make up a movie.

The way that numbers are used to represent the information in a media file is called the file *format*. There are several formats for audio files and several more for video. Each format uses a unique formula to determine the order and meaning of each number that is used to represent audio and video.

You will need to know which file formats the Player uses, what the files contain, and which file format will play most effectively for your situation. For example, if you are surfing the Web and are given a choice of whether to download and play a WAV file or a WMA file, knowing what each format means can make quite a difference. WAV files are very large but reproduce sound exactly the way it was recorded. WMA files are much, much smaller in size, but lose some quality when they are played. You may not be able to tell the difference in sound quality, but if you have a slow Internet connection, you'll know the difference between a half-hour download and a two-minute one!

Determining file types with extensions

Microsoft Windows stores files by giving them names. Each file name has an *extension* that is used to determine the file type. File name extensions are created by putting a period after the file name and adding three letters. An example of a file name extension would be the ".wma" portion of the file named "laure.wma".

By default, the extension of a file name is hidden by Microsoft Windows Explorer. For Windows 98, you can make extensions visible in the **Folder Options** dialog box, which you can access on the **View** menu. When the **Folder Options** dialog box appears, click the **View** tab, and then clear the check box labeled **Hide file extensions for known file types**. Now Windows Explorer will show file names complete with their extensions. Figure 3.1 shows the **View** tab with extensions not hidden. If you are using a different version of Windows, consult the online help for directions on how to show file name extensions.

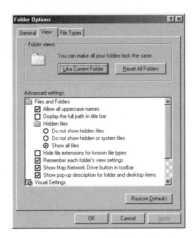

Figure 3.1 – *View tab of the **Folder Options** dialog box.*

When you double-click a file to play it, Windows looks at the file name extension to determine which application will process the file. For example, if a file name extension is ".wma", Windows Media Player will start up and play the file.

Changing file associations

You can change which application will process files that have a particular extension. For example, Microsoft Notepad is the default text file editor that comes with Windows, but you can tell Windows to run another text editor instead. Deciding which application to run for a particular file name extension is called *file association*. You can change the file association of a particular extension by going to the **File Types** tab of the **Folder Options** dialog box, which you can reach from the **View** menu of Windows Explorer in Windows 98. Click the file type you want to change, click the **Edit** button, and supply the information needed to tell Windows which application you want to run. Figure 3.2 shows the **File Types** tab for Windows 98. If you are using a different version of Windows, consult the online help for directions on how to change file associations.

Figure 3.2 – *The **File Types** tab of the **Folder Options** dialog box in Windows Explorer.*

Changing file associations in Windows Explorer is a somewhat difficult process and not recommended for beginners. Windows Media Player has a much easier way to help you make sure that all music and video files are played by the Player. The best way is to install Windows Media Player and not install any other types of audio or video players.

During the installation of the Player, you'll be asked which file types you want Windows Media Player to play, and all you have to do is select all the options as shown in Figure 3.3.

Figure 3.3 – *Setting file associations during installation of the Player.*

If you didn't select the option of playing all media files when you installed the Player, you can always change your options by going to the full mode of the Player and choosing **Options** from the **Tools** menu. When the **Options** dialog box is displayed, click the **Formats** tab and select all the check boxes of the file types you want Windows Media Player to play. See Figure 3.4.

Figure 3.4 – *The **Formats** tab of the **Options** dialog box in the full mode Player.*

Warning! If you install other media players on your computer, the file name extensions may be changed without your knowing it. You can always have Windows Media Player change the extensions back, of course. Windows Media Player provides the best listening and viewing experience for all the file formats it supports, but you may want to prove it to yourself by trying out other players.

Supported file types

Windows Media Player 7 supports the following file types. This section discusses each type in this order:

- Windows Media metafiles

- Windows Media audio

- Windows Media video

- Windows Media download

- Windows video

- Windows audio

- MPEG movie

- MP3 audio

- MIDI

- Indeo video

- AIFF audio

- AU audio

- CD audio track

Windows Media metafiles

Meta is a Greek word that means "next to" or "nearby". A metafile is a special type of file that describes or gives more information about another file. Windows Media metafiles have the following extensions.

Extension	Description
.asx	Contains information about .asf files. The extension .asf was used for both audio and video files by previous versions of Windows Media.
.wax	Contains information about audio files. When you save an audio playlist, the Player will use this file format.
.wvx	Contains information about video files. When you save video playlist, the Player will use this file format.

Metafiles are text files that use XML (Extended Markup Language) to define specific kinds of information. Metafiles provide several ways to enhance the Player.

Using metafiles for playlists

The most popular use of metafiles is as the file format for reading and writing playlists on your hard disk. If you create a playlist, and you want to save it for later or send it to a friend, Windows Media Player will use a metafile to store the playlist information. You can learn more about playlists in Chapter 13.

Using metafiles for borders and advertising

You can use metafiles to insert advertising that will be played with an audio or video presentation. You can also use metafiles to link content to skin-like borders and create a multimedia experience. For more information about inserting advertising and using the Windows Media Download file format, see Chapter 13.

Using metafiles for captioning

If you want to provide captions or subtitles for video files, you can put the text for the captions into a metafile. You can even provide captions in several different languages in the same file so that the user can choose which language they want to see. For more information about captioning, see Chapter 13.

Using metafiles for streaming media

If you are sending out audio or video that is being broadcast live, you can use metafiles to create announcement files. An announcement file specifies when the broadcast will take place and on what channel. By loading the announcement file ahead of time, the Player can start receiving the file at the appropriate time. For more information about streaming media, see Chapter 4.

Windows Media audio files

Windows Media audio files have the following extensions.

Extension	Description
.asf	Contains audio information. This format was used in previous versions of Windows Media.
.wma	Contains audio information.

The two formats are identical except that the second format is audio only, while the first can contain audio or video information.

Windows Media video files

Windows Media video files have the following extensions.

Extension	Description
.asf	Contains video information. This format was used in previous versions.
.wmv	Contains video information.

The two formats are identical except that the second format is video only, while the first can contain audio or video information. Video files can also contain audio information as a separate track contained in the same file.

Windows Media download files

Windows Media download files contain a skin and media that can be used to create multimedia applications using Windows Media Player. The contents of the Windows Media download file are compressed and consist of one or more media files, a skin, and a metafile. The file name extension is .wmd.

By compressing audio or video content along with a skin and defining the relationship of the content and skin with a metafile, the Windows Media download file can link audio, video, artwork, and Web sites together easily. For more information about Windows Media download files, see Chapter 13.

Windows video files

Microsoft Windows has a native video file format with the .avi extension. It contains video information and usually an audio track in the same file.

Windows audio files

Microsoft Windows has a native audio file format with the .wav extension. It contains audio information only.

MPEG movie files

Movies created to the specification of the Moving Picture Experts Group (MPEG) can have the following file format extensions:

.mpg

.mpeg

.mpe

.m1v

.mp2

.mpa

.mpe

The Moving Picture Experts Group is a committee that creates standards for audio and video. Each standard is numbered. The MPEG movie file standard is also known as MPEG-1. For more information about MPEG movies, see the official Web site at:

http://www.cselt.it/mpeg/

MP3 audio files

MP3 files are audio files created according to the Moving Picture Experts Group (MPEG) standard known as Audio Layer 3. This file format uses the file name extension .mp3 or .m3u.

For more information about MPEG audio, see the official Web site at:

http://www.cselt.it/mpeg/

MIDI files

MIDI stands for Musical Instrument Digital Interface and is not an audio or video format. It is a programming protocol that defines a method for musical instruments to connect to computers and to each other. MIDI files use the extensions .mid, .midi, and .rmi.

Part of the MIDI specification defines a file format that can store musical information about notes and other programming information. Unlike audio and video files that store the exact digital information to reproduce sounds and pictures on a computer, MIDI files only contain generalized data. For example, a MIDI file might contain the musical notes for a song and specify that the notes be played on a piano. Because a MIDI file is more of a mathematical description of a song than sounds, MIDI files can be very small. A note on a scale is very simple. The actual data to reproduce sounds is very complicated.

Windows Media Player can play MIDI files. The exact sounds associated with particular notes may be different on each computer, depending on the sound cards used. For more information about MIDI, see the MIDIFarm Web site at:

http://www.midifarm.com/

Indeo video files

The Indeo video file format uses the file name extension .ivf. Indeo was recently acquired by Ligos Technology. For more information about the Indeo video file format, go to the Ligos Web site at:

http://www.ligos.com/indeo/intel.shtm/

AIFF audio files

The Audio Interchange File Format (AIFF) is one of the most popular file formats for the Apple Macintosh computer. This format uses the .aif, .aifc, and .aiff file name extensions. For more information about AIFF, see the Apple Computer, Inc. Web site at:

http://devworld.apple.com/techpubs/mac/Sound/Sound-61.html

AU audio files

The AU audio file format uses the .au file name extension. The .snd sound file format is very similar. Both of these formats are popular on UNIX and UNIX-type computers. For more information on these formats, see:

http://www.cica.indiana.edu/cica/faq/audio/audio.html#unix

CD audio track files

Windows Media Player will play music CD tracks. The CD track extension is .cda.

Codecs

A codec is the formula used to convert audio and video into digital formats. The word *codec* is a combination of the two words "compressor" (co-) and "decompressor" (dec). A codec is needed because most audio and video is compressed when it is converted into digital form and decompressed when it is played. Often codecs are associated with particular file formats, but a file format may work with more than one kind of codec. In addition, new versions of codecs are always being created. If you want to play a file, you must have the same codec with which the file was encoded.

Codecs use a variety of techniques to compress a file. Standard mathematical formulas are used as well as new concepts in compression that look at how you hear music and see video. Music compression is particularly interesting because some frequencies of the music can be deleted without the listener being aware. For example, if a piece of music is mostly drum and bass, you can cut out the high frequencies and never know what you are missing. Or if a particular passage is mostly high notes, you can cut out the lower frequencies. You can also remove frequencies that the human ear cannot hear. By analyzing the sounds carefully, the codec formula can be very efficient at reducing the size of a file.

Sampling and Bit Rates

When audio is compressed by using a specific codec, a formula is used. During the compression process, the amount of compression can be chosen. There are three main ways to measure the kind of audio information in a file: sampling rate, bit rate, and stereo/mono.

Sampling rate

The sampling rate determines the maximum frequency range that is stored in the file. The greater the frequency, the more data that is stored and the more realistic the sound will be. Typical sampling rates will range from 8 kHz (telephone quality) to 44.1 kHz (CD quality). A typical Windows WAV file might be stored at 22.1 kHz.

Bit rate

Besides the range of frequency, the other measure of sound stored in a file is the bit rate, which is the number of bits of data that represent a second of sound information. Higher bit rates mean greater fidelity, but also mean larger file sizes. Bit rates are often referred to as 8-bit (8K bits per second) or 16-bit (16K bits per second). A typical WAV file would be recorded at a 16-bit rate.

Stereo or mono

Finally, whether the data is stored in stereo or mono will determine whether there are two tracks of data. If stereo, there will be twice as much information stored per second and the file will be twice as large.

File quality

The sampling rate, bit rate, and whether it is stereo or mono will determine the total quality of the file in pure technical terms. However, the codec formula used will determine the quality of the sound experience. Two files compressed at the same sampling and bit rates will sound very different if different codecs are used. The psychology of how humans hear music and speech is very different from the mechanical measurement of frequency and bits per second.

Using MP3

WAV files can be very large. For example, a 10-second WAV file stored in stereo at a sampling rate of 22.1 kHz with a 16-bit rate will be 778 KB (796,800 bytes) in size. Depending on your Internet connection, it may take longer than 10 seconds to download. But once you start working with codecs, the file size can shrink.

One of the most popular codecs in the past few years is MP3, which is the Moving Picture Experts Group Audio Layer 3 codec. (For more information about MP3 files, see the section called "MP3 files" earlier in this chapter.) If you compress the 778 KB WAV file using an MP3 codec, the file size will drop to only 23.8 KB. This is at a bit rate of 20 Kbps and you will be able to tell the difference in sound. But if you use a higher bit rate, say 64 Kbps, the file size will only be 78 KB. The file size will be only a tenth of the original, but the sound quality of the MP3 file will be almost as good as the original WAV file and you may not be able to tell the difference. What might have taken you a minute to download on a slow Internet connection will take you only a few seconds.

Using the Windows Media Audio codec

As good as MP3 is, Windows Media has a new codec that is even better. The Windows Media audio codec can compress files so that they sound even better than MP3 files at the same bit rate and as good as MP3 at lower bit rates.

What this means is that if you have a 78 KB MP3 clip recorded at 64 Kbps, you can now have a WMA file that will sound as good, but will only take up 41 KB when recorded at 32 Kbps.

Besides offering a smaller file size for the same audio quality, Windows Media audio codec has another advantage as well. When the Windows Media audio codec is used to create Windows Media files with the .wma extension, those files can be streamed. Streaming lets you listen to a file without downloading it first. For more information about streaming files, see Chapter 4.

Where do you get codecs?

One of the best features of Windows Media Player is that you don't need to worry about codecs at all. When the Player opens a media file, it looks to see what kind of codec it needs. If the proper codec is not already on your computer, the Player will ask you if you'd like to download the codec. If you say no, you can't play the file; but if you say yes, Windows Media Player will do all the work for you (assuming you have a connection to the Internet).

You can set an option in the Player to not even ask you whether you want to download new codecs. If you click **Options** on the **Tools** menu and then click the **Player** tab in the **Options** dialog box, you can select the check box that says **Enable automatic codéc download** as shown in Figure 3.5.

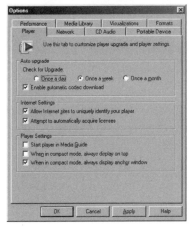

Figure 3.5 – *Setting the Player to automatically download codecs.*

Because new codecs are always being invented to compress music into smaller and smaller files while making it sound better, using Windows Media Player will guarantee that you're always up-to-date. Codecs are relatively small because they are formulas, so downloading a new codec only takes a minute or two, and is much easier than downloading a whole new Player.

Which codecs do you have?

If you'd like to see which codecs you have installed on your computer, all you need to do is go to **Control Panel** in Windows 98 and use the Multimedia Control Panel to display the Multimedia Devices list in the **Multimedia Properties** dialog box. A typical Multimedia Devices list for Windows 98 is shown in Figure 3.6. If you are using another version of Windows, consult Windows Help for details.

Figure 3.6 – *Checking your codecs.*

Click **Audio Compression Codecs** to see a list of audio codecs, and click **Video Compression Codecs** to see the video codecs. You'll see a big list of codecs that were initially installed with Microsoft Windows, codecs installed by Windows Media Player, and perhaps other codecs installed by other programs.

Figure 3.7 – *Audio Compression Codecs.*

If you'd like to know more about a particular codec, double-click it to bring up a dialog box. For example, if you want to see more about the MP3 codec, it will look something like figure 3.8.

Figure 3.8 – *MP3 codec dialog box.*

Notice that this dialog box gives you several options, none of which you are likely to ever want to use. You can do the following types of things with codecs: change their priority, temporarily disable them, remove them, or just find out more about them.

If you think you're having a problem with a codec, you can temporarily re-move it by clicking **Do not use this audio codec**. Later, you can always click **Use this audio codec** if you want to bring the codec back.

You can also change the priority of a codec. If you have two similar codecs, and the wrong one is being used, you can change their priorities so that the codec you want will be used instead.

And if you're sure you don't want a particular codec, you can remove it by clicking on the **Remove** button. You might want to do this if you're trying to install a newer version but the old one is blocking it.

You're not likely to need any of these options, but they are good to know about if you are having codec problems. If you want more information about the creator of the codec, you can click on the **About** button to display an information box. Figure 3.9 shows the **About** dialog box for the MP3 codec.

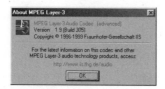

Figure 3.9 – *The **About** dialog box for the MP3 codec.*

Understanding digital rights

Due to the vast improvements in streaming media and compression technology, high quality audio and video are a reality on the Web. Digital rights management systems in combination with other technology offer content providers and retailers a flexible platform for the secure distribution of digital media files. This digital content can be easily copied and distributed without reduction in quality. Consequently, music and video artists, publishers, and other content providers face serious problems with protecting their rights to the digital content. This book will not attempt to address the issues of infringing copyrights or violating the law, except to say that music, video, and other types of content are protected by certain rights, and the technology described in this book is not intended to be used to violate those rights. For example, the technology described in this book may help you to access content, make copies, transfer content, or add or remove settings, but it is your responsibility to ensure that you have the legal rights to such uses of the content.

> **Note**   Any unauthorized use of content subject to such rights and/or licenses may be a violation of the law, including U.S. and international copyright laws, and may subject you to civil and criminal prosecution.

Creating encrypted music files

Windows Media has a solution that's simple and works to help protect the rights of content owners while enabling consumers to easily and legitimately obtain digital content. Microsoft Windows Media Rights Manager enables the artist, publisher, or authorized distributor of music to define how the file can be used, and control the rights that are given to consumers.

A Windows Media encrypted file can be set up so that it can only be played a few times before it expires. Or it can be set up so that it can only be copied from one computer to another so many times. This allows the content provider to control fees for music licensed over the Internet, and it's good for you because this will encourage content providers to make more music available over the Internet. There are several different ways that Windows Media digital rights work.

The process of tracking digital rights involves the use of a license. Windows Media Rights Manager not only encrypts the music, it also gives that music a unique number and creates a license for it.

Downloading songs

Using Windows Media rights management, you can pay for a song and download it to your computer or digital device. The song has been encrypted, is in Windows Media Format (with a .wma extension), and has a unique ID number. When you start to play your new song on Windows Media Player, the Player will go to a secure Web site and confirm that you are the registered licensee of that particular copy. If you are, license information will be placed on your hard disk. You can then play the song according to the terms of the license. For example, some licenses may allow you to play the song a limited number of times, or just for a period (for example a 30-day demo), or it might give you rights to play the song for any duration and as many times as you like.

Windows Media Player (or any player that licenses the Windows Media technology) has a feature that is designed to play the encrypted files only if the license is present. License information is unique to a particular computer, and the content is encrypted to play only on that computer.

If you decide to sell your computer or reformat your hard disk, Windows Media Player can help you move the licenses to another computer.

Streaming a video

You can also use Windows Media digital rights to view a secure video. After you pay the appropriate fees (if any), the video can be streamed to you. A license is issued to you, but because you are watching the video live and not storing it on your disk, the license will delete itself after the video ends.

Listening to previews

Windows Media digital rights can also be used to let content providers give people a preview of their works. For example, using Windows Media Rights Manager, the content provider could set up each file so that it can only be played twice. If you try to play it a third time, Windows Media Player wouldn't let you do it, but would take you to a Web page where you could pay for the file, assuming that the content provider wanted it to work this way.

Subscribing to a music Web site

A service could be created where music owners, publishers, or other content providers could sell subscriptions. For example, for a fixed fee, a consumer could download all the music they wanted for a month. At the end of the month, the music would expire and new licenses could be issued by renewing the subscription.

Similarly, music could be rented for a specific period. Consumers could pay a small amount if they only wanted to listen to a song for a month, but pay extra if they wanted the song for a year. Windows Media Player has a feature that will keep track of the rights you buy as a consumer and make the content available to you accordingly.

Managing licenses

You can manage the licenses on your hard disk by clicking **License Management** on the **Tools** menu of the full mode Player.

Figure 3.10 – *The License Management dialog box.*

The dialog box shown in Figure 3.10 enables you to determine where you want your license information stored on your hard disk. If part of your hard disk becomes corrupted, you can restore your licenses provided that you backed them up first. All you need is a connection to the Internet, and the information can be copied back down to your computer. This provides a secure way to keep track of all the music you have licensed for your personal use, without worrying about accidentally losing it.

Copy settings enable personal rights management

Windows Media Player includes features that can help you create on your computer your own personal mix of your favorite music files from CDs. For more information about copying music from a CD, see Chapter 2.

By default, the Player encrypts the files you create and creates a license for them on your computer. If you try to copy the music to another computer without moving the license, the encrypted files won't play and you will see an error dialog box similar to Figure 3.11.

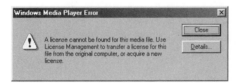

Figure 3.11 – *Missing-license error dialog box.*

You can click the **Details** button of the dialog box for more information.

You can turn off the encryption of files by clicking **Options** on the **Tools** menu and then clicking the **CD Audio** tab. If you clear the check box labeled **Enable Personal Rights Management**, the music you copy from a CD won't be encrypted.

However, if you don't use personal rights management, you may not be able to copy your files to a portable device such as a Pocket PC. For more information about copying music to portable devices, see Chapter 5.

Copying music to a CD

Copying music from your computer to a CD is called *burning*. The process of creating your own CD is very simple: create a playlist of the songs you want to copy, and then burn the songs onto the CD.

Create a playlist

The first thing you need to do is decide what music you want to put on your CD. Create a new playlist, and give it a name you'll remember. Then choose the songs you want to put on your CD and pick the order of the songs. Figure 3.12 shows a playlist called "My Faves" with several different songs.

Figure 3.12 – *Playlist example.*

Push the button

After you've decided on a playlist of songs to copy, click **Copy to CD** on the **File** menu of the full mode Player. You'll be given a list of playlists. Pick the one you created in the previous step. Figure 3.13 shows the dialog for picking the playlist of songs you want to burn.

Figure 3.13 – *Dialog box that lets you select a playlist to copy to a CD.*

If you select a playlist that is less than 10 minutes total playing time, you'll be asked if you want to burn a CD anyway. Because Windows Media Player closes off the recording session at the end of the copy sequence, you are being notified that you won't be able to add any other tracks after the session closes. You can tell the Player not to ask you again by selecting the check box in the dialog box. Figure 3.14 shows the warning dialog box.

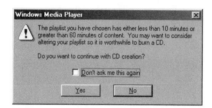

Figure 3.14 – *Warning if less than 10 minutes.*

Next, the Player checks to see what drives you have and whether one of them is a CD recorder. If you do not have a CD recorder, you will get an error message similar to Figure 3.15.

Figure 3.15 – *Error message if your computer does not have a CD recorder.*

If you do, the Adaptec Easy CD Creator Plug-In will ask you to insert a recordable CD (CD-R) into the drive. Click the **Start** button to begin recording. Figure 3.16 shows the CD copying dialog.

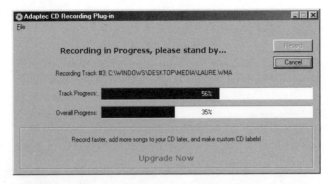

Figure 3.16 – *Progress of copying files to a CD.*

The copying process should take only a few minutes.

CHAPTER 4

Receiving Internet Audio and Video

This chapter covers the three ways that Windows Media Player can receive audio and video over the Internet. The World Wide Web is a collection of millions of computers all tied together with a network. Information is sent through the network in the form of *packets*. A packet is a small fixed unit of data. Packets are like envelopes sent through the mail. Each packet has an address it is being sent to, an address it came from, and some content.

Windows Media Player can receive audio and video from the Internet in three ways:

Downloading a file

You can download a file from a Web site. When you've finished downloading, you can play the file on Windows Media Player. Choose this option if you want to keep the file.

Progressively downloading a file

You can play an audio or video file from a Web site. The Player will download small parts of the file and play it as it goes along. Choose this option if you just want to listen to a file. The file will only be kept on your computer temporarily.

Streaming

You can receive an audio or video stream from a Web site. The site must be set up to stream content that has been prepared by Windows Media Technologies. The audio or video will start playing right away. There is no file involved, only a stream of bits is received. The Player can automatically choose the best quality stream to use.

Downloading files

When files are downloaded from the Internet, the file data travels from a sending computer (called a *server*) to a receiving computer (called a *client*).

How files are transmitted

The transmission follows a standard process:

The file is broken down into packets.
The sender takes the file and converts it to small chunks called *packets*. Each packet is numbered and has a destination address.

The packets are sent to the network.
The connection between computers can be a wire, fiber optic cable, radio wave, or even infrared light beams. Like clerks in the back room of a post office, hardware *routers* guide the packets to their destination. Each computer connected to the network has a fixed address, known as the *IP address*. (IP stands for Internet Protocol. A *protocol* is a formula for doing things, and the Internet Protocol is a way to define addresses so that each computer is unique.)

Routers pass the packets through the network.
Because the Internet is a complex and crowded system of possible connections, routers decide which way to route a particular packet, based on network loads. If one path is full, the router will choose another. Often the packets that make up a particular file follow different routes and sometimes don't arrive in the same order they were sent.

Packets arrive at the receiver.
When packets start arriving, the receiving computer starts keeping track of which packets have arrived and which have not. Because the packets can be sent along different routes, the receiver will wait a reasonable time before sending a message to the server asking for the missing packet to be sent again.

Packet are converted to a file.
When all the packets are received, the receiving computer converts them into a file. If any missing packets didn't arrive after a reasonable amount of time, an error message will be displayed to the user of the computer.

How to download a file

You will usually have the opportunity to download a file when you encounter a link to a file in a Web page. To download the file from Internet Explorer, right-click the link and click **Save Target As**. Figure 4.1 shows the shortcut menu you will see.

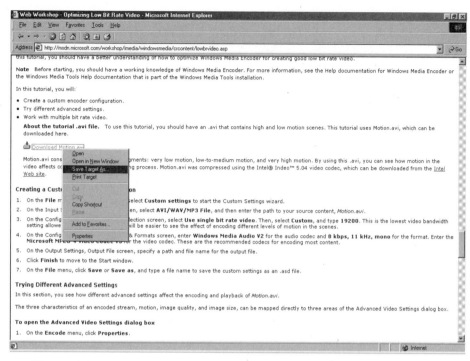

Figure 4.1 – *Shortcut menu with the Save Target As option selected.*

When you select the option, the **File Download** dialog box appears. See Figure 4.2 for the **File Download** dialog box.

Figure 4.2 – *File Download dialog box.*

After enough of the file has been loaded for the Windows operating system to analyze it, you will be asked where you want to put the file on your computer. Figure 4.3 shows the **Save As** dialog box.

Figure 4.3 – *Save As dialog box.*

After you have chosen a location, you will see a dialog box showing the progress of the download.

Figure 4.4 – *File copying progress dialog box.*

After the file is finished copying, it will be stored on your hard disk. You can play it with Windows Media Player the same way you would play any other audio or video file on your computer.

Progressive downloading

Music and video files can sometimes be quite large. It can be frustrating if it takes you a long time to copy a file from the Internet, and then after you play it, you discover that you don't like it. Windows Media Player gives you the ability to begin playing a file right away instead of waiting.

The technology for copying files from the Internet is the same as for progressive downloading. The difference for progressive downloading is that as soon as the Player gets enough packets, it will begin playing the audio or video file. Almost instantly you'll be able to hear the music or see the video. Figure 4.5 shows the Player receiving a file through progressive downloading.

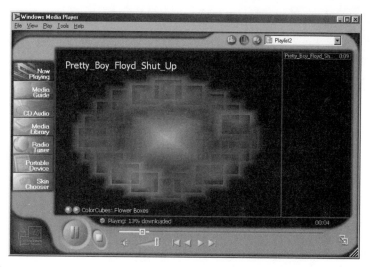

Figure 4.5 – *Progressive downloading of a file from the Internet.*

You can see that 13% of the file has been progressively downloaded, both by the text at the bottom of the **Now Playing** view, and by the position of the white strip in the seek bar. The thumb is slightly behind the white strip, indicating that the music is playing.

It is important to understand that progressively downloading a file does not copy the file to your disk in the same way that a normal download does. You will not be asked for a location to copy the file to. A copy of the file may be temporarily saved, but it will be erased whenever your temporary Internet file cache is flushed. For more information about temporary files, see Internet Explorer Help.

If you have a slow Internet connection, the Player may not be able to download the packets as fast as it can play them. The Player gathers packets and waits until it has enough of them. The amount it gathers before attempting to play is called a *buffer*.

File buffering

A buffer is a temporary holding place for computer data. A single packet doesn't contain enough data to display a frame of video or enough audio to play something you will recognize. Windows Media Player takes the packets it receives and puts them into a buffer. When the buffer is full, the Player takes the data out of the buffer and begins playing the content. Then, while the content is playing, the Player begins filling the buffer again, with new data that's coming in. Each time the buffer is filled, the Player takes the data from the buffer and adds it to the content that will be played.

You can adjust the buffer size of the Player from the **Performance** tab of the **Options** dialog box of the Player. See Figure 4.6 for the **Performance** tab of the **Options** dialog box.

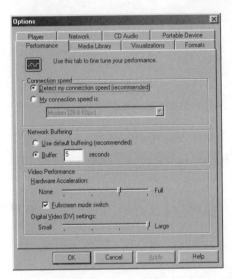

Figure 4.6 – *Performance tab of the **Options** dialog box.*

If you are having problems with buffering and the Player isn't able to keep up with a slow network connection, you can change the buffer size. The buffer size is measured in seconds. The larger the buffer, the longer you will wait before the Player will start playing a section of the file being progressively downloaded.

Streaming media

Streaming media is the transmission of audio and video from one computer to another. Sound and visual images are encoded into computer data and transmitted over the network as a stream of bits. The receiving computer takes the bits and assembles them into sound and visual images that the user can listen to and watch. Files are not copied; no files are involved. Only streams of packets are sent and received.

Multiple versions of the same media can be broadcast simultaneously so that the Player can automatically choose which version will give the best quality for your network connection. This is called *intelligent streaming*. Streams can be encoded at different bit rates; the bit rate is related to the amount of computer data that represents one second of audio or video. The higher the bit rate, the better the quality of the media. Intelligent streaming allows streams encoded at different bit rates to be combined into one stream. When the Player receives a broadcast that was prepared for intelligent streaming, it will automatically choose which stream to play based on your Internet connection, giving you a better audio and video experience.

A stream can be live or recorded. If it is live, you can set up the Player to tune in and start playing when the show starts. If it is recorded, you can get it whenever it's convenient.

Receiving live broadcasts

You can tune into a live broadcast very easily. The Web site that will broadcast the event sets everything up for you. All you need to do is click a link that goes to an announcement file. After the Player receives the announcement, it will analyze the information and get ready to play. If the broadcast has already started, the Player will begin in the middle of the broadcast. Otherwise, it will wait until the broadcast is scheduled to begin. At the time of the broadcast, the Player will start playing.

Announcement files

Announcement files have the extension .asx, .wax, or .wvx. An announcement file is created when a file is encoded by Microsoft Windows Media Encoder; they can also be encoded manually because they are text files that use the XML protocol. Announcement files are also known as Windows Media metafiles. Metafiles serve many purposes for Windows Media technology and you can read more about them in the Windows Media Player 7 SDK, which is on the companion CD of this book.

Receiving recorded broadcasts

If you tuned in too late for a broadcast, you may be able to get it again later. Usually a Web site will provide a link to a recorded versions of a broadcast. Click the link and the Player will receive the stream as if it were live. Packets will begin streaming to your computer and you can see whatever you missed.

Unicast and multicast streams

There are two types of streaming media. The most prevalent type is called *unicast* and delivers media streams from a server to each computer individually. Windows Media also is able to send out *multicast* streams, which are similar to radio and television broadcasts. All computers can receive the stream at the same time.

Unicast streams

Most streaming is done by unicast. A server sends out packets to each computer that requests a stream. Figure 4.7 shows a diagram of a unicast.

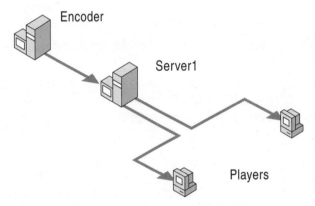

Figure 4.7 – *Unicast streaming.*

Unicast is a good way to receive live broadcasts, but it does have its drawbacks. The server must send out streams individually to everyone who wants to receive the broadcast. If you only have a handful of people receiving the streams, this is fine. But if you're trying to send broadcasts out to thousands of people, there are two drawbacks with the unicast process.

Too many requests

With unicasts, the server has to process each person's stream and send it out. Each stream takes a tiny bit of processing power. If you get too many requests, the server can't keep up with the processing workload, and some people won't receive the broadcast. This is the same problem that file servers have. If you've ever tried to download a file that everyone else is trying to download, you've run into this situation. Sometimes, if a server gets too many requests, it not only won't fill all the requests, it might even stop working entirely.

Too many packets

The second problem with unicasts to large numbers of people is that a separate set of packets must be sent out to each person. Even if the server can do this, the number of packets flooding out for a big broadcast can slow the whole system down. Packets on the Internet are like cars on a highway. If you start sending too many packets out, the whole Internet slows down, just like a freeway at rush hour.

Receiving multicasts

Multicasts use a new form of networking. Instead of sending out streams from a single server to a single client, a multicast sends out a single set of packets which can be received by everyone. This requires almost no server load and very low Internet traffic. The unicast process is similar to the way that telephones work, that is, information is broadcast from point to point. In the early days of telephones, people had the idea of using telephones to broadcast music, but the switching nightmare made it clear that this wouldn't work. Then radio and television came along, and they are similar to multicast. One set of information is sent out, and many radios or televisions receive the program.

Tuning in

All packets move through a network at high speeds. They are directed by routers until they find the address they are intended for. A computer watches the network and grabs any packets addressed to it. It converts the packets to useful information and marks the packets so they won't be passed on by any more routers.

With multicast, your computer is set up so that in addition to listening for packets addressed to it, it also listens for packets that are addressed to a multicast-specific address, called a station. Multicast reserves a set of addresses for broadcasting that cannot be assigned to any computers. If your computer is set up for multicasts, it will listen for packets on a particular station. When it receives a packet on that station, it converts the packet into useful information and passes it along to Windows Media Player to be played. At the same time, all the other computers receiving the broadcast are getting the same packets from the same station.

Multicasts are very efficient. A single set of packets can be used to broadcast to the entire Internet. Figure 4.8 is a diagram of a typical multicast.

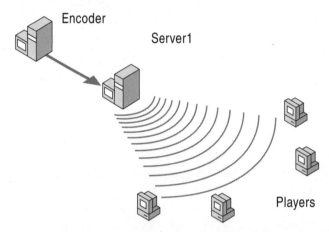

Figure 4.8 – *The multicast process.*

Receiving multicasts

From the user's point of view, receiving a multicast is the same as receiving a unicast. You click a link to an announcement file, the Player is set up correctly, and at the proper time, the Player opens and plays the audio or video you want. The only difference is that the server won't crash, you know you'll get the broadcast you want, and the whole Internet will be less crowded as more multicasts are used.

Because a multicast is broadcast by sending out one set of packets, there's no easy way to have the Player request that a missing packet be sent again. This may mean that some packets are lost, but a certain number can be lost before you notice it, due to the way that Windows Media files are encoded.

To receive a multicast, you must enable the Windows Media Player for multicasts. If you have difficulty receiving a multicast on the Player, click **Options** on the **Tools** menu, and then click the **Network** tab of the **Options** dialog box. Be sure the **Multicast** check box is selected. See Figure 4.9 shows the **Network** tab of the **Options** dialog box.

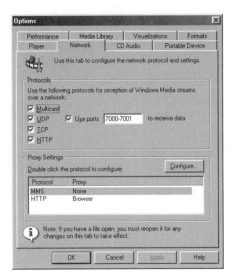

Figure 4.9 – *The **Network** tab of the Player **Options** dialog box.*

While multicasting might be the long-term solution to network traffic jams on the Internet, we're not there yet.

Multicasts have not yet replaced unicasts on the Internet because some parts of the Internet aren't connected by routers that understand the multicast process. Most new routers can handle multicasts just fine, but older government and educational systems that link pieces of the Internet are using outdated equipment. On the user end, most network cards on recent computers also understand multicasts. But the issue will remain for at least another year or two until the remaining gaps (known as clouds) are modernized.

There is one area where multicasts are becoming very popular. Multicasts work very well on corporate intranets. If your corporation uses Windows Media Technologies, the chances are that it uses the multicast method, because it saves network resources and keeps network loads lighter. This is an ideal way to broadcast training and company-wide communications. Multicasts are also being used in geographical areas that don't have any clouds. For example, a multicast can be sent out successfully to a large city.

Multicasting is clearly going to play an ever-growing role in the future of the Internet. But no matter what the future brings, you can receive an ever-changing, ever-growing assortment of audio and video from the Web. You will have a choice between simple downloads, progressive downloading, and streaming. Each choice has its advantages, but as Internet connections become faster, streaming will become more common. Ultimately, you may not need to keep audio and video files on your computer, you may be able to stream anything you want at any time of the day or night. And no matter how you choose to receive files from the Internet, Windows Media Player can take care of the details and play what you want, the way you want it.

CHAPTER 5

Using Windows Media Player with Portable Devices

The first four chapters of this book discussed the personal computer version of Windows Media Player. This chapter will introduce you to a new, smaller Windows Media Player that works on the Pocket PC. You'll also learn how to use Windows Media Player to load music onto the smaller Player and how to give it new skins.

Using portable devices

Computer users live in a world that gets more portable every day. The first computers were the size of rooms and needed huge amounts of energy to keep them powered and even more energy to keep them cool. Computers moved to the desktop but were still not easy to carry from place to place. Laptops soon came in but still required a place to put them down. Only recently have computers shrunk down small enough to be carried in your pocket.

Music in your pocket

The Internet music revolution makes it possible to download music to your personal computer and then copy it to a portable music device. These tiny devices, not much larger than a pack of playing cards, let you take music with you everywhere, and listen to it on headphones.

You can use Windows Media Player to download music from the Internet and then put it on a portable device such as a Creative NOMAD or an S3 Rio. Devices like these will play hours and hours on a set of batteries. Unlike tape or CD players, a portable music player won't skip or wear out fast, because there are no moving parts except for the buttons.

A further advantage of using Windows Media Player with a portable music player is that you can use the Windows Media Format for your music files.

Earlier portable music players operated only with the MP3 (MPEG Audio Level 3) music format, but many newer players are enabled for the Windows Media Format. This is a big improvement because Windows Media files are much smaller than MP3 files but sound just as good or better. For more information about file formats, see Chapter 3.

Newer portable music players can take advantage of the Windows Media Format. Two players that are available now are the NOMAD II from Creative Labs (Figure 5.1) and the S3 Rio 600 (Figure 5.2). For more information about the NOMAD II, see the Creative Labs Web site at:

http://www.creativelabs.com/

For more information about the Rio 600, see the S3 Web site at:

http://www.s3.com

Figure 5.1 – *NOMAD II portable music player from Creative Labs.*

Figure 5.2 – *Rio 600 portable music player from S3.*

PC in your pocket

The newest portable computer is the Pocket PC. The Pocket PC is powered by Windows and is built and distributed by a variety of manufacturers. Figure 5.3 shows four different Pocket PC brands.

Figure 5.3 – *Four different brands of the Pocket PC.*

The Pocket PC is so small and lightweight that it fits right in your pocket, and you can carry it everywhere. It has many of the capabilities of a full-size computer, but you can hold it in your hand. Instead of typing on a keyboard, you tap on the screen with a stylus to input words, draw, or play games.

The Pocket PC is much more than a simple personal information manager. It is a real computer running Microsoft Windows. A typical Pocket PC runs at 131MHz, has 32MB of RAM, contains a bright screen with 65,536 colors, and plays clear audio sound. The Pocket PC will look familiar to you because it uses the Windows user interface; however, because you tap on the screen with a stylus instead of using a mouse, the interface has been redesigned to be easier to use in a small area. For more information about the Pocket PC, see the Pocket PC Web site at:

http://www.pocketpc.com/

Here is a list of some of the things you can do with the typical Pocket PC:

- Surf the Web. Using Pocket Internet Explorer, you will be able to plug into a modem or network connection and download Web pages.

- Get your email. You can plug your Pocket PC into a modem, network, or wireless device and send and receive mail through your Pocket Inbox.

- Keep all your personal information and synchronize it with your desktop personal computer. You can store all your contact, calendar, and task information on your Pocket PC. Then, whenever you want, you can update your data by using a cable or infrared port to copy information back and forth between your Pocket PC and your desktop computer.

- Use Microsoft Word, Microsoft Excel, and Microsoft Access. Smaller versions of these applications are included with the Pocket PC. You can use Pocket Word, Pocket Excel, and Pocket Access on the go and copy the results to and from your desktop computer.

- Read books. Now you can take a book with you. Taking advantage of the new Microsoft Reader with ClearType technology, you can download books and read them clearly even on the 2-inch by 3-inch screen.

- Record notes to yourself. You can press a button and talk. The Pocket PC will record your voice, and you can play it back later. It's very handy for memos in the car or while out walking.

- Carry it with you. The Pocket PC fits in a pocket, purse, or briefcase. You can even clip it to your belt. Imagine a 3-inch by 5-inch card that's half an inch thick; that's how big it is.

- Not have to buy any more batteries. A Pocket PC has a rechargeable battery that typically provides about six hours of continuous use. That's enough to last all day because you're probably not going to be using it every minute, though you may use it more than you think!

All these features come standard with the typical Pocket PC. In addition, you can install hundreds of other applications. You can use products such as Expedia to help keep you from getting lost, applications like Microsoft Money to keep track of your finances, and the Microsoft Game Pack for those long plane trips.

You can connect your Pocket PC to the world by using a variety of additional devices. A CompactFlash slot enables you to connect phone modems, wireless modems, and network cards easily. You can even connect your cell phone to a Pocket PC and surf the Web from the wilds of the woods.

If you use a serial CompactFlash card, you can connect cameras, GPS (global positioning system) devices, bar code readers, and a host of other hardware devices.

Windows Media Player for Pocket PC

There's one more feature that comes standard with every Pocket PC: Windows Media Player for Pocket PC! Now you can take your music with you, no matter where you go. Just transfer your favorite music from your desktop personal computer to your Pocket PC by using the **Portable Device** feature of Windows Media Player 7. Figure 5.4 shows Windows Media Player for Pocket PC.

Figure 5.4 – *Windows Media Player for Pocket PC*

Using Windows Media Player on a portable device

This section focuses on using Windows Media Player for Pocket PC, but if you have an earlier Windows CE device, you may be able to download Windows Media Player for Palm-size devices. For information, see the Windows Media Web site at:

http://www.windowsmedia.com/

Starting the Player

You don't have to install Windows Media Player for Pocket PC on your portable device. It is already installed and appears on the main menu. To start the Player, just tap the **Start** menu at the top left of the screen and then tap **Windows Media**. The main view of Windows Media Player for Pocket PC will appear. (Figure 5.4)

Using the buttons

Unlike the desktop Windows Media Player, Windows Media Player for Pocket PC has only a few buttons and controls. It can still do more than you might think, but everything starts from the main view (Figure 5.4). Table 5.1 shows the buttons and their functions.

Button	Function
▶	Toggle between **Play** and **Pause**.
◼	**Stop**.
▸▸	Go to the **Next** song in the playlist.
◂◂	Go to the **Previous** song in the playlist.
↻	**Repeat** the current item in the playlist.
⤨	**Shuffle** the order in which the playlist items will be played for this session. This does not change the absolute order of the playlist, just the playing of items in the list.
ⓘ	Display an **Information** dialog box about the current item in the playlist
◁	Toggle between a muted (sound off) and un-muted (sound on) state.

Table 5.1 – *Button functions of Windows Media Player for Pocket PC.*

Using the sliders

In addition to pushing buttons, you can move the sliders on the Player to change the volume and position of the currently playing audio.

The volume slider is at the bottom of the screen and looks like Figure 5.5. Drag the thumb button to the left to make the Player quieter and drag it to the right to make it louder.

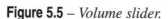

Figure 5.5 – *Volume slider.*

The audio will start playing at the beginning of the song. You can make the song start anywhere you want by moving the thumb button of the track navigation slider. The left end of the slider represents the beginning of the song, and the right end represents the end of the song. The track navigation slider looks like Figure 5.6 and is at the top of the screen.

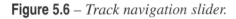

Figure 5.6 – *Track navigation slider.*

Copying music to and from your devices

If you want to listen to more than "Welcome to Windows Media" on your Windows Media Player for Pocket PC, you need to copy music from your personal computer to your Pocket PC. Copying music is easy. Earlier chapters of this book told you how to find music on the Internet and copy music from CDs to compile playlists on your personal computer. After you have your music ready to go and in a playlist, just click the **Portable Device** tab of the full mode Windows Media Player. It should look like Figure 5.7 (assuming a Pocket PC is connected to your computer).

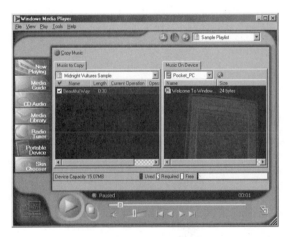

Figure 5.7 – *Portable Device view of Windows Media Player.*

On the left you see the contents of a playlist; in this case it is the default song that comes with Windows Media Player 7. On the right is the current musical content of a Pocket PC, showing the default audio file that comes with a Pocket PC. Below the two panes is a narrow pane that shows the device capacity (in this case, 15.07MB), and a horizontal bar graph showing how much is free (white), how much is used (blue), and how much will be used by the amount of music selected in the left pane.

When you're ready to copy the music, click the **Copy Music** button near the upper left. You should see a screen similar to Figure 5.8, showing that the copying has started.

Figure 5.8 – *Copying music from a personal computer to a Pocket PC.*

When you are done, the screen should look like Figure 5.9.

Figure 5.9 – *Copying is complete.*

You'll notice that on the left, the check box is no longer selected and the word "Complete" is displayed in the Current Operation column. On the right you'll see that two songs are now loaded into the Pocket PC.

Note that there is a **Select All** button above the check boxes that looks like a check mark. By clicking this button, you can select all boxes below. Click it again to clear all boxes. This can be very efficient when you only want to copy a few selections. Deselect all selections, and then click the boxes of the few you want to copy.

Deleting songs from the Pocket PC

You can delete a song on your Pocket PC from either the Pocket PC or the Windows Media Player.

You can delete a file directly from your Pocket PC with the following steps:

1. From the main menu of your Pocket PC, open **File Explorer**.

2. Find the file you want to delete, and tap and hold on the file name.

3. On the pop-up menu that appears, tap **Delete**.

You can also delete files on your Pocket PC indirectly from Windows Media Player on your desktop personal computer by clicking the song name in the right pane of the **Portable Device** view. See Figure 5.10 for an example of deleting a file by using Windows Media Player.

Figure 5.10 – *Deleting a file remotely.*

After you delete the file, the view should look like Figure 5.8. If want to verify that the file is really gone, you can use the Mobile Device folder on your personal computer to verify that it is gone. The Mobile Device folder is a listing of all the files on your Pocket PC. Figure 5.11 shows a Mobile Device folder that corresponds to the Pocket PC contents shown in Figure 5.9 (with one new file and one old). Figure 5.12 shows the Mobile Device folder after the new file has been deleted.

Figure 5.11 – *Contents of the Mobile Device folder showing the new file added.*

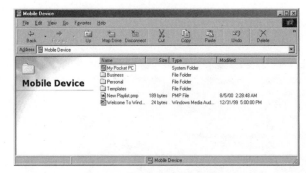

Figure 5.12 – *Contents of the Mobile Device folder showing that the new file has been deleted.*

Files that can be copied

The following types of audio files can be copied from your computer to a Pocket PC:

- Windows Media files with a .wma extension

- Windows Media files with an .asf extension (Video portions will not be copied.)

- MP3 files (but they will be converted to Windows Media files)

Digital rights management

Chapter 3 discussed digital rights. You must have a license for any copy-righted music you want to copy to a portable device that supports digital rights management.

Furthermore, without a license, you won't be able to copy an audio file from a portable device that supports digital rights management to a personal computer that supports digital rights management. For more information on digital rights management, see Chapter 3.

In order to copy music from your personal computer to a Pocket PC or portable music player that supports digital rights management, you must enable the personal rights management feature of the personal computer version of Windows Media Player 7. To do so, use the following steps:

1. On the **Tools** menu, click **Options**.

2. In the **Options** dialog box, click the **CD Audio** tab.

3. Select the **Enable Personal Rights Management** check box.

Figure 5.13 shows the **CD Audio** tab of the **Options** dialog box.

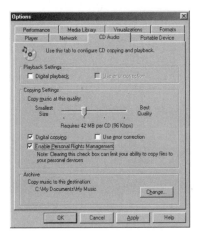

Figure 5.13 – *CD Audio tab of the Options dialog box.*

Optimizing file copying

You can decide the quality of the audio files that will be copied to your portable devices. If you're short of space on your portable device, you can have the files you copy converted to a lower bit rate by using the **Portable Device** tab of the **Options** dialog box. Figure 5.14 shows the **Portable Device** tab.

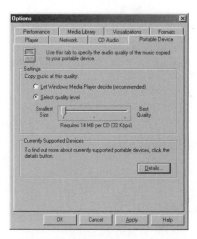

Figure 5.14 – *Portable Device tab of the Options dialog box.*

Using the **Portable Device** tab, you can choose to let Windows Media Player decide on the best course of action, or you can choose for yourself and use the slider to get the results you want. Slide it all the way to the left for the smallest files (which won't sound as good) and all the way to the right to get the best sound but the biggest file sizes. The slider gives you an indication of the size tradeoff by telling you how much space (in megabytes) the music on a CD would require on a portable device.

Creating playlists on a portable device

You read about playlists for Windows Media Player in Chapter 2, but using playlists is much simpler with the Pocket PC. If you select **Playlist** at the bottom of the screen (see Figure 5.4), you'll see a new screen that looks like Figure 5.15.

Figure 5.15 – *Playlist on a Pocket PC.*

You can work with the current playlist by using the icons at the bottom of the screen. The following actions are initiated by those icons:

Green plus sign

Adds a song to the current playlist.

Red X

Deletes the selected song from the playlist.

Up arrow

Moves the selected song up one position in the playlist.

Down arrow

Moves the selected song down one position in the playlist.

Solid arrow that points right

Returns to Windows Media Player. You can also do this by tapping the **OK** button at the top right corner of the screen.

You can select a different playlist by tapping the **New Playlist** menu at the top of the screen. You will have the option of choosing another playlist, or a special playlist named **All My Music** that contains all the music on the device, or a new screen called **All Playlists.** From the **All Playlists** screen, you can create new playlists, rename playlists, or delete playlists you no longer want.

Using skins on portable devices

Just like the desktop Windows Media Player, Windows Media Player for Pocket PC lets you use and create skins.

Loading skins

You can load skins by using the **Skin Chooser** portion of the Windows Media Player for Pocket PC Fun Pack. You'll want the Fun Pack because it has extra features for your Pocket PC. For more information, go to the Pocket PC Web site at:

http://www.pocketpc.com/

When you are using the Fun Pack to install additional applications, be sure to include the **Skin Chooser** option. Figure 5.16 shows the screen you'll use to install the **Skin Chooser** on your Pocket PC.

Figure 5.16 – *Installing the **Skin Chooser** option.*

After you install the **Skin Chooser**, you can use it to install skins on your Pocket PC. Figure 5.17 shows a typical **Skin Chooser** session in action.

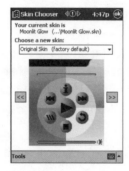

Figure 5.17 – *Skin Chooser*.

Creating your own skins

You can create your own skins for the Pocket PC by following the instructions in the Windows Media Player for Palm-sized and Pocket PCs SDK, which can be obtained from the Microsoft Web site at:

> *http://www.microsoft.com/windowsmedia/*

Using other portable devices

Almost everything in this chapter that talks about using the **Portable Device** feature of Windows Media Player applies to other portable devices, not just Pocket PCs. If you're using another portable device, the main difference is the name of the device under the **Music On Device** drop-down list box. Some features may not apply.

Part 2
Creating Skins

CHAPTER 6

What Are Skins?

This chapter will introduce you to the basic programming concepts of creating skins. It will cover the architecture of skins and show how the technologies of XML, Microsoft JScript, and artwork can be combined to make skins. Chapter 7 will go into more detail about how you can design a skin, and Chapter 8 includes a step-by-step procedure that will show you how to put together all the element of a sample skin. Chapter 9 will give you advanced skin techniques and Chapter 10 will explain how to test skins.

Introduction

Skins are a revolutionary new technology that lets you change the look and feel of Windows Media Player. Now you can create custom artwork that will look and function almost any way you want. The possibilities are endless.

First you'll be shown the basic visual modes of the Player and skins. You'll need to familiarize yourself with each mode in order to build skins. When you start the Player and click **Now Playing**, the Player will look something like Figure 6.1. This is called the full mode of Windows Media Player.

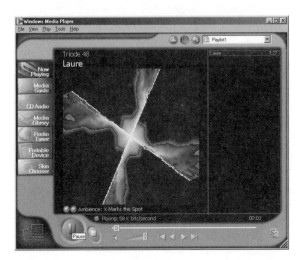

Figure 6.1 – *Full mode of Windows Media Player.*

If you choose **Compact Mode** from the **View** menu, you'll see a skin, not the full mode view. It's important to know the difference between the full mode and the compact mode of the Player, because skins only run in compact mode, and there are important differences in functionality between the two modes.

If you have never loaded a skin before, and you choose compact mode, the default skin will appear. The default skin of the Player looks like Figure 6.2.

Figure 6.2 – *Windows Media Player in compact mode showing default skin.*

The default skin is similar to the full mode Player in that it has all the transport controls to play, pause, stop, and so on. Skin designs will often hide some controls by putting them in a sliding drawer. Here are two examples of how that can work.

If you click the button that sticks out of the right edge of the default skin, a drawer will slide out showing the current playlist. Figure 6.3 shows the playlist drawer of the default skin.

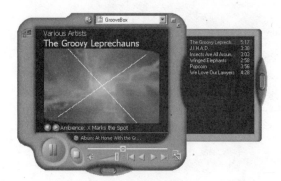

Figure 6.3 – *Playlist drawer of the default skin.*

If you click the button that sticks out of the bottom of the skin, you'll see the settings drawer slide out. Figure 6.4 shows the settings drawer.

Figure 6.4 – *Settings drawer of the default skin.*

Skin art can be very complex. It can be large or small, and as full-featured as the skin designer wants. The default skin looks a lot like the full mode Windows Media Player, but there are hundreds of new and original skin designs that you can apply to your Player. For example, you can have a skin that looks like Figure 6.5.

Figure 6.5 – *Headspace skin.*

Architecture of skins

A computer user interface is the combination of what you see on a computer screen and how you interact with it by clicking your mouse or typing on the keyboard. A skin is a customizable user interface for the Player.

Windows Media Player provides a customizable user interface for several reasons:

- Skins let people use the Player the way they want to. You can design what buttons are used, where they are, and what happens when you push them.

- Skins contain unique artwork that can be used for advertising and promotion. You can promote your band, Web site, or favorite charity. "Click here and buy our new CD!"

- Skins are fun! Are you tired of the way the Player looks? There are so many skins out there that you could have a new one nearly every day and never run out.

Skins drive the player

Skins provide one or more controls that let the user interact with the engine of the Player. A careful look at this interaction will help you understand how the user, the skin, and the Player work together.

The flow of interaction is shown in the following steps:

- A user clicks a **Play** button with a mouse.

- The click is routed through the computer to Microsoft Windows.

- Windows analyzes the click and determines that you clicked the portion of the screen that is owned by Windows Media Player.

- Windows notifies the Player that one of its buttons was clicked.

- The Player determines what the button click means and selects what to play.

- The Player instructs Windows to play the music, and Windows notifies the hardware to start the music.

- The user hears the music coming out of the computer speakers.

Skins are art

Without art you won't have much to look at in a skin. Skins can be created from text alone, but you're most likely to want to use art to give a skin a unique look. Because there are so many types of art creation programs, you can find one that works with your skill level. You can use clip art, or draw your own images, or do anything in between. You can even use photographs to enhance a skin.

You'll get a better overview of what kinds of art you need later on in this chapter under the heading "Art files". Chapter 8 will go into detail on how to create the art you need for a sample skin using the art program Adobe Photoshop.

You'll have to create one or more art files, and they will be the face that the world sees when people use your skin. You don't necessarily need formal art training or expensive art programs. Skins have been created using the program Microsoft Paint which comes with Windows. All that is required is the willingness to learn, the ability to follow directions, and a little creativity!

Skins are code

Even if you have the most elaborate and beautiful work of art in the world, it won't make a good skin unless you add some software coding to process the keystrokes and mouse clicks. Fortunately, you don't need to be an expert programmer to make great skins.

Skin programming is done in two languages: XML and Microsoft JScript. These languages work together and are complementary. XML is used to define the characteristics of each button, slider, and text box. JScript isn't always necessary, but often will be used to provide added functionality. You'll learn more about XML and JScript in later sections of this chapter.

Skin programming and Web page programming are very similar. If you have done any programming with Web pages, you'll feel right at home with skins, because XML is very similar to HTML. JScript is widely used in Web programming and is similar to other scripting languages such as Perl and Microsoft Visual Basic Scripting Addition (VBScript).

One of the things that makes Web programming easy is that you can see how a Web page is put together by viewing the source code. Skins work the same way. You can take apart any skin and look at how the art and the code work together. By examining other people's skins, you can build up a library of coding techniques that you can use again and again. A Skin file is really a set of files compressed into one file with the file name extension .wmz. All you have to do is unzip the skin file to see all the files contained inside.

XML

The first part of skin programming that you must understand is how to work with XML. If you've used XML elsewhere, you'll still need to see how Windows Media Player uses XML, because every implementation of XML is different. XML is used to define the basic building blocks of the user interface for skins.

What is XML?

XML stands for Extensible Markup Language and is one of the newest techniques used for Web technologies. Essentially, XML is very similar to HTML (Hypertext Markup Language) except that it is extensible; that is, you can define new parts of the language as you go along. For skins, you don't need to worry about the details of XML. You won't be creating new XML codes, only using the ones provided by Windows Media Player. If you'd like to know more about XML, see the Microsoft's MSDN Web site at:

http://www.msdn.microsoft.com/xml/.

How XML is used in skins

In skins, XML defines a set of buttons, sliders, and text boxes; all of them make up the user interface of the skin. Each piece of the user interface is called an element. The elements are defined by tags, which are simple keywords that are enclosed by angle brackets. For example, the **BUTTON** element is defined by the **BUTTON** tags, which look like this:

```
<BUTTON>
</BUTTON>
```

The opening tag and the closing tag are the same except that the closing tag has a forward slash after the left bracket.

Often there will be some extra code between the tags. For example, you might have a **BUTTONGROUP** element that includes two buttons.

```
<BUTTONGROUP>
    <BUTTON>
    </BUTTON>
    <BUTTON>
    </BUTTON>
</BUTTONGROUP>
```

You can define an element by giving it attributes. For example, you can give a button a name that you can refer to later.

```
<BUTTON  name  =  "mybutton">
</BUTTON>
```

Sometimes if there are no elements inside a set of opening and closing tags, you can skip the closing tag and use a forward slash before the right angle bracket.

The rules of XML

XML has a few simple rules that you need to know to create skins. XML requires you to follow the rules exactly. The rules are as follows:

Enclose element tags with angle brackets

All element tags are enclosed by angle brackets; for example, the **BUTTON** element is typed

```
<BUTTON>
```

You do not need to type the word "BUTTON" in all capital letters, but the convention of typing element names in all capitals is used in the example code throughout this book.

Put attributes before the closing bracket

All attributes for a particular element must be included before the closing angle bracket of the opening tag. An attribute consists of the attribute name followed by an equal sign (=) and the value of the attribute in quotation marks. For example,

```
<BUTTON  image  =  "soup.bmp">
```

You do not need to type the word "image" in lowercase, but the convention of typing attribute names in lowercase is used in the example code throughout this book.

Use opening and closing element tags

Some elements are grouped together inside another element. For example, the **BUTTONGROUP** element does not make a lot of sense unless you use one or more **BUTTONELEMENT** elements with it. To make the grouping clear, you need to have an opening and closing tag for each element. The opening tag is just the element name and any related attributes, surrounded by angle brackets. The closing tag is the element name, preceded by a forward slash (/), and then enclosed by angle brackets. For example, the **BUTTONGROUP** element opening tag is:

```
<BUTTONGROUP>
```

and the closing tag is:

```
</BUTTONGROUP>
```

You would put the **BUTTONELEMENT** tags between the opening and closing **BUTTONGROUP** element tags. For example:

```
<BUTTONGROUP>
    <BUTTONELEMENT   />
    <BUTTONELEMENT   />
    <BUTTONELEMENT   />
</BUTTONGROUP>
```

Close off elements

If an element has no other elements inside it, you can put a forward slash at the end of the element name just before the closing angle bracket of the tag. For example, in the code above, each **BUTTONELEMENT** tag has a forward slash to indicate that there are no other elements nested within it.

In other words, you must either have a closing element tag or close off your element with a forward slash at the end of the opening tag.

This is correct:

```
<BUTTONGROUP>
    <BUTTONELEMENT   />
    <BUTTONELEMENT   />
</BUTTONGROUP>
```

This is not:

```
<BUTTONGROUP/>
    <BUTTONELEMENT   />
    <BUTTONELEMENT   />
</BUTTONGROUP>
```

The following is also incorrect because the **BUTTONELEMENT** tags are not closed off.

```
<BUTTONGROUP>
    <BUTTONELEMENT>
    <BUTTONELEMENT>
</BUTTONGROUP>
```

How to author in XML

You don't need a sophisticated editing environment to author in XML. You can create XML files with a text editor. You can use any editor you like as long as it saves to straight text files. If you use a word processor like Microsoft Word, be sure that you are using a **Save As** option that uses a text-only format (do not use Rich Text or Doc format). However, if you start doing a lot of skin coding, you may want to use a professional development environment like Microsoft Visual InterDev, which provides advanced editing and debugging features.

All of your XML skin code goes in one file, known as the *skin definition file*. This file is the traffic coordinator of your skin. The file contains the basic instructions for what the skin does and where the other pieces are. There can only be one skin definition file for a skin, and it must have the extension .wms (Windows Media Skin). If the skin definition file and related files are collected and compressed into one ZIP file, the extension is .wmz (Windows Media Zipped).

How to create the Skin Definition File in XML

All you have to do to create the skin definition file is define the elements you want to use in the skin. If you want a few buttons, add some **BUTTON** elements. Want a slider? Add a **SLIDER** element. After you code your elements, define them with attributes. You're done!

It's not quite that easy, but almost. One thing you'll need soon is the Windows Media Player 7 Software Development Kit (SDK). It's on the companion CD that comes with this book. You'll want to load both the Player itself and the SDK. The SDK covers every skin element and attribute and also comes with several working skin examples you can study. The companion CD also contains a Skins Construction Kit with art and code you can use for making skins easily.

Skins can be very simple. Here's a simple skin definition file that uses XML to create all the code that is needed to start and stop the Player.

```
<THEME>
    <VIEW
        clippingColor   =   "#CCCC00"
        backgroundImage   =   "background.bmp"
        titleBar  =  "false">

            <BUTTONGROUP
                mappingImage   =   "map.bmp"
                hoverImage   =   "hover.bmp">

            <PLAYELEMENT
                mappingColor   =   "#00FF00"  />

            <STOPELEMENT
                mappingColor  =  "#FF0000"  />

        </BUTTONGROUP>

    </VIEW>
</THEME>
```

This the minimum code needed to create a two-button skin. The two buttons are **Play** and **Stop**. You'll also notice that there's a lot of white space, and if you look at the code, you'll see that it follows the rules of XML.

But looking at the code doesn't help you very much, even if you know the rules of XML. It's like knowing the grammar of a spoken language but not the vocabulary. You need to know what words you can use and how the words relate to each other.

XML structure

The skin definition file must follow a specific structure. You start with a **THEME** element, create one or more **VIEW** elements, and then define each **VIEW** element with the user interface elements appropriate for the type of **VIEW** you want to use. Then you add specific elements to each view, such as buttons, sliders, text boxes, and so on.

Theme

At the top level, you must start the skin definition file with the **THEME** ele-ment and close with it.

```
<THEME>
    . . .
</THEME>
```

The **THEME** element is the root element for your skin. There can be only one **THEME** element in a skin definition file, and it must be at the top level. **THEME** elements have specific and ambient attributes, though most of the time you will not need to use them. For more information about the attributes of each element, see the Windows Media Player 7 SDK, which is on the companion CD included with this book.

View

Each theme must have at least one view. The view governs the particular image you see on the screen. You may want to have more than one view, so you can switch back and forth. For example, you might want to have a large view for working with playlists, a medium view for watching visualizations, and a tiny view that fits in a corner of the screen. If you are creating multiple views, you will want to be sure that each view has a unique **id** attribute value that will be used to identify it when called from code.

Each **VIEW** element can also have one or more **SUBVIEW** elements. A **SUBVIEW** element is similar to a **VIEW** and can be used for parts of your skin that you want to move around, hide, or show. For example, a **SUBVIEW** element might be used to create a sliding tray that pops out of your skin to display a graphic equalizer. A **SUBVIEW** can be aligned with the **VIEW** and have other special relationships to the **VIEW**.

Other UI elements

After you have defined your **THEME** and **VIEW** elements, you must populate your **VIEW** with specific user interface elements. You do not have to use all the available elements in a skin, just the ones you need.

If an element can be seen by the user, it is called a control. The following controls are available for skins:

- Buttons

- Sliders, custom sliders, and progress bars

- Text boxes

- Video windows

- Visualization windows

- Playlist windows

- Subview windows

In addition, the following elements can be used to further define Windows Media Player actions, but they require visual elements such as buttons or sliders:

- Video settings

- Equalizer settings

- Visualization settings

Buttons

Buttons are the most popular part of a skin. You can use buttons to trigger actions such as play, stop, quit, minimize, and switch to different view. Windows Media Player provides the skin creator with three types of button elements: the **BUTTON** element, the **BUTTONGROUP** element, and several predefined button elements.

BUTTON element

The **BUTTON** element is used for stand-alone buttons. If you use the **BUTTON** element, you must supply an image for each button and define the exact location, in pixels, where you want the button to appear, relative to the background image. One of the advantages of the **BUTTON** element is that you can change the button image dynamically.

BUTTONGROUP element

The **BUTTONGROUP** element is used for groups of buttons. You must enclose each **BUTTONGROUP** element with a set of **BUTTONGROUP** tags. Using button groups is easier than using individual buttons because you do not have to specify the exact location of each button. Instead, you supply a separate mapping image that defines the actions that will take place when the mouse hovers over or clicks an area on your background.

Predefined buttons

There are several predefined buttons. Each one is the same as a regular button except that some of the attributes have already been filled in for you. For example, you can use a **PLAYELEMENT** button to play media files and **STOPELEMENT** button to stop. See the Windows Media Player SDK for details.

Sliders

Sliders are useful for working with information that changes over time. For example, you might use a slider to indicate what part of a media file the Player is currently playing. Sliders can be horizontal or vertical, linear or circular, or any shape you can think of. Sliders come in three varieties: sliders, progress bars, and custom sliders.

Sliders

You can use the **SLIDER** element for volume controls or to allow the user to move to a different part of the media content.

Progress bars

Progress bars are similar to sliders. Progress bars are designed for displaying information that changes, but not data that the user will want to interact with. For example, you might want to use a progress bar to indicate buffering progress.

Custom sliders

A custom slider is provided so you can create controls such as knobs, or do unusual control mechanisms. For example, if you want to create a volume control that wraps around your skin, you can do it with a custom slider. To set up the custom slider, you must create a mapping image that contains grayscale images to define the locations of the values on the slider. This is relatively easy to do with an art program that has layers.

Text

You can use the **TEXT** element to display text on your skin, such as song titles.

Video

You can display video in your skin. The **VIDEO** element allows you to set the size and position of the video window.

You can also allow the user to change the video settings with the **VIDEOSETTINGS** element. For example, you can create controls to adjust the brightness of the video.

> **Note** If you do not supply a **VIDEO** element, and the content contains video, Windows Media Player will return to full mode and your skin will not be displayed.

Equalizer Settings

You can set the filtering for specific audio frequency bands by using the **EQUALIZERSETTINGS** element. Essentially this means you can boost the bass, tweak the treble, and set up your sounds to match your ears or your living room.

Visualizations

You can display visualizations in your skin. Visualizations are visual effects that change with the music that is playing through Windows Media Player. The **EFFECTS** element determines where the visualizations will play, what size the window will be, and which visualizations will be played.

You can also use the **EFFECTS** element to define how custom visualizations are displayed. For more information about creating custom visualizations, see Chapter 14.

Playlists

You can use the **PLAYLIST** element to allow the user to select an item from a specific playlist.

Subviews

You can use the **SUBVIEW** element to display secondary sets of interface controls, such as playlist or video controls.

JScript

You can create very nice skins using only XML to define the user interface elements. However, eventually you're going to want to make the Player do more than just play. In order to add real programming power to your skins, you'll need to use Microsoft JScript. At first you can add simple lines of code here and there to do certain tasks, and soon you'll be wanting to do more. There are dozens of books on how to use JScript (which is similar to Netscape JavaScript but is not the same as the Sun Microsystems Java or Microsoft J++ programming languages).

You can add lines of JScript to your XML code to perform certain tasks. For example, to close a view named **myView**, you could type:

```
<BUTTON
    onclick = "JScript: myView.close() ;"
 . . .
 >
```

The actual JScript code is treated as an attribute of a particular **BUTTON** element. (The rest of the button attribute code is not shown.)

Calling JScript functions

If you need to call more than a few lines of code, you can load a script file using the **scriptFile** attribute of the **VIEW** element, and call the functions in the script. You can load more than one file per view; for example:

```
scriptFile = "myfile1.js ; myfile2.js ; myfile3.js"
```

After the script files are loaded, you can call functions in them from inside your View section. For example, to call a function called **myfunction** when something is clicked, type:

```
onclick = "JScript: myfunction()"
```

> **Note** If you have more than one view, only the functions in files loaded into the current view are available to the XML and JScript code running with the current view. Files loaded in other views are not in the same scope (memory space) with the current view. Because they are in a different scope, attributes from one view are not readable in another.

Controlling the Player

Aside from the XML that you write to initialize attributes for your skin, the primary code you write is JScript code to tell Windows Media Player what to do. For example, a typical command might be:

```
player.URL  =  "file:laure.wma"
```

JScript is an object-oriented language, and **player** is an object. Windows Media Player has an object called **player**. Objects are packages of code that have methods, properties, and events associated with them. The **player** object has a property called **URL**. After **URL** is assigned a value, the **player** object will start Windows Media Player playing whatever file the URL is pointing to. A URL (Uniform Resource Locator) is a protocol for finding files on a network

Windows Media Player is controlled from JScript by calling methods, assigning values to properties, or responding to events. You can learn more about methods, properties and events by reading any book on Microsoft ActiveX technology, because Windows Media Player uses an ActiveX control to allow itself to be controlled by JScript in a skin.

If you are confused by the intertwining of XML and JScript in skins, remember the following two ideas. Objects that define the user interface are defined in XML and use elements and attributes. You can think of these as passive objects. The ActiveX objects control the Player and have methods, properties, and events. You can think of them as active, for ActiveX.

Reading and writing properties

You can send information to Windows Media Player through JScript by assigning values to properties. You can also receive information through properties. You've just seen how the Player responded to being sent a value for the URL property. An example of receiving information from the Player is getting the current status of the Player by using the **status** property. The code would look like this.

```
Text.value  =  player.status
```

If you had a text box on a skin, you could assign it the value of the status of the Player. The object is **player** and the property is **status**. **Text** is an object also, but this is because it is an XML element and all elements are objects to

JScript. **Text** has an attribute of **value**; all attributes are the same as properties to JScript. The assignment is from right to left, which means that the information contained in the property **status** is copied to the property **value**. Property names are separated from object names by a period.

Calling methods

You can get the player to take action by calling a method. For example, if you want to close Windows Media Player, use the following JScript code:

```
player.close()
```

The object is **player** and the method is **close**. Methods are also separated from their objects by a period, and methods must be followed by parentheses.

The **player** object contains several other objects. Because Windows Media Player has so many options, one object would be too many. For example, the **player** object has a **controls** object inside it. You can get to the **controls** object through the **controls** property of the **player** object.

Responding to events

Events are either external or internal; external events come from the user, and internal events come from Windows Media Player.

External events

When users click a button or press a key, your skin can respond to their input with event handlers. An event handler is a section of code that runs whenever the event is triggered.

The following external events are supported by skins:

- **click**
- **close**
- **dblclick**
- **error**
- **keydown**
- **keypress**

- **keyup**

- **load**

- **mousedown**

- **mousemove**

- **mouseout**

- **mouseover**

- **mouseup**

- **resize**

- **timer**

See the Windows Media Player 7 SDK for more details about specific events.

A typical external event handler names the event and defines the code that will run. For example, if you want to create code to start Windows Media Player when the user clicks a button, put a line similar to the following in your button code.

```
onclick = "JScript: player.URL = 'file:laure.wma' ;""
```

This will play the file named laure.wma when the button is clicked. Note that you add the word "on" to specific event names when defining an event handler.

Internal events

You can detect changes that occur in Windows Media Player or changes in your own skin. These can be changes in properties or methods of Windows Media Player objects, changes in skin attributes, and so on.

Windows Media Player property changes

You can process changes in Windows Media Player by using the **wmpprop** listener. You must set up the listener as a value of an attribute. Put the value in double quotes, and start with the word **wmpprop** followed by a colon. Then include the property you want to listen to. When the property changes, the value of the attribute will change also. For example, to have a slider element value change whenever the value of the **currentPosition** attribute changes, type the following:

```
<SLIDER    id="mySlider"    value="wmpprop:player.Controls.currentPosition"/>
```

Important Do not use **wmpprop** on Windows Media Player methods. Unexpected results may occur.

Windows Media Player method changes

You can make your skin respond to the availability of methods on Windows Media Player by using **wmpenabled** and **wmpdisabled**. These are used similarly to the **wmpprop** listener except that you can only use these on methods of the **Controls** object that are supported by the **isAvailable** method. See the Windows Media Player 7 SDK for more information about **wmpenabled**, **wmpdisabled**, and **isAvailable**.

For example, you could enable a button only when the **Play** method is enabled, using code like this:

```
<BUTTON ... enabled = "wmpenabled:player.Controls.Play();" />
```

Important Do not use **wmpenabled** or **wmpdisabled** on Windows Media Player properties. Unexpected results may occur.

Skin attribute changes

You can respond to changes in your skin attributes in one of two ways, by using **wmpprop** or the **_onchange event**.

You can use **wmpprop** to listen for changes in your own skin. For example, to show a slider value in a text box, type the following:

```
<TEXT ... value = "wmpprop:mySlider.value">
```

You can use the **_onchange** event to process events inside an element. You must attach the name of the attribute you want to track to **_onchange**. For example, if you want to track the value of a text box, type:

```
value_onchange
```

and then assign a JScript string that you want to run when the value changes. For example, to respond to a change in the value of a text box that can be used to adjust the volume of Windows Media Player, type the following inside your Text control as an attribute:

```
value_onchange = "JScript: player.Settings.Volume = myText.value"
```

Writing event code

Events are similar to attributes in the way they are coded. You must give the event a value, and the value is the code you want to run when the event happens. The word "on" is added to the front of the event name; for example, the **click** event will become **onclick**.

The event value is in double quotes and starts with the word JScript followed by a colon. The code you want to run comes next, followed by a semicolon and the closing double quotes. For example, to stop playing when the user clicks a button, type the following as an attribute in your **BUTTON** element code:

```
onclick = "JScript: player.Controls.Stop() ;""
```

If you have a code that requires quotes, use single quotes. Care must be taken when using quotation marks so that they are balanced properly. Here is an example of using both types:

```
onclick = "JScript: player.URL = 'file:..\\laure.wma' ;""
```

You can also change attributes of your skin when handling an external event. For example, to close a view named **myView**, type:

```
onclick = "JScript: myView.close() ;"
```

Secondary events

You can determine what other events are taking place when a specific event is triggered. For example, when a mouse button is clicked, you may want to know whether the ALT key was down at the same time.

Event Attributes

The following event attributes are supported for skins:

- **altKey**
- **button**
- **clientX**
- **clientY**
- **ctrlKey**

- **fromElement**

- **keyCode**

- **offsetX**

- **offsetY**

- **screenX**

- **screenY**

- **shiftKey**

- **srcElement**

- **toElement**

- **x**

- **y**

For more information about these attributes, see the Skin Programming Reference section of the Windows Media Player SDK documentation.

Using secondary events

You can only process event attributes in JScript code. You must use the syntax

```
event.eventattributename
```

where eventattributename is the name of the event attribute. For example, to determine whether the ALT key was down during a click event, you could use the following lines in your JScript code:

```
wasAlt = event.altKey ;
if (wasAlt = "True") ...
```

Art files

You must create one or more art files for your skin. There are three types of art used in skins:

Primary image
  You must create a primary image for your skin. This is what users will see when they install your skin. The primary image is composed of one

or more images that are created by specific interface elements. If you have more than one element, you must specify the z-order. It defines which elements are displayed "in front" of other ones.

Each **View** control will have a background image that you can add other element images to, allowing you to create a primary composite image. You also may have secondary images, such as a sliding tray, that do not display when your skin first appears, but that show up when the user takes some action. These follow the same rules as primary images, in that they are created with a set of controls.

Mapping images

One of the most powerful features of Windows Media Player skins is that you can use mapping images to trigger events for your skin. Mapping images are files that contain special images. The images in a mapping image file, however, are not meant to be viewed by the user, but are used by Windows Media Player to take action when the user clicks a button or other control on your skin. In essence, the user cannot see mapping images, but the mouse can.

Different elements need different kinds of mapping images. For example, if you color part of a mapping image a specific red value, and the user clicks the corresponding area of your primary image, the button that is at the corresponding location will fire an event. Color is used to define which events are triggered by clicks in what areas of the skin. This may sound odd, but it allows a great deal of artistic control over the actions that your skin can process.

Alternate images

You can also set up alternate images to display when a user does something. For example, you can create an alternate image of a button that will be displayed only when the mouse hovers over the button. This is a good way to let users know what they can do, and also allows for a highly discoverable user interface. By using ToolTips and hover images carefully, you can create unusual user interfaces that still give the user feedback on what options are available.

Art file formats

The following art file formats are recognized by Windows Media Player and can be used for creating skins:

BMP

Bitmap images are recommended because they offer the most control over the exact image and colors.

JPG

Compressed image format used for Web pages.

GIF

Compressed image format used for Web pages. Animated GIFs are supported.

PNG

Compressed image format used for Web pages.

> **Note** If you use one of the compressed file formats that defines a color as transparent to a Web browser, do not define a color as transparent in the image file. Use a visible color to represent transparent areas in your image, and then define that color as transparent in the skin definition file instead of the image file. For example, if you create a .gif file with some areas transparent, they will not be transparent in your final image and you will not be able to use the color you set as transparent in your .gif file as the transparency color in your skin.

Simple art example

Three art files are needed to create a simple skin with two buttons: a primary image, a mapping image, and an alternate image.

The art files in the following example were created in Adobe Photoshop, but any art program could be used. An art program that uses layers is easier to work with because you will want to be sure that your primary, mapping, and alternate images are all the same size and line up with each other.

Primary image example

The primary image for this example skin is a simple yellow oval with two buttons, a pink one to start Windows Media Player and purple button to stop it. The background is a slightly darker yellow than the oval. Figure 6.6 shows the simple background image.

Figure 6.6 – *The primary image background.*

The primary image was created in Adobe Photoshop from the following images, each in a separate layer. First an oval was created with a layer bevel and emboss effect. Figure 6.7 shows the primary image oval.

Figure 6.7 – *The primary image oval.*

Then the two buttons were created, also with layer bevel and emboss effects. Figure 6.8 shows the two buttons.

Figure 6.8 – *Two primary image buttons.*

Next the color mask for the primary image was created. A color mask value defines the areas in your skin that will be transparent and let the desktop show through. A slightly darker yellow was chosen so that any mixing of pixels between the oval and the background will blend in seamlessly. The color value is #CCCC00. This number is shown in the Photoshop **Color Picker** dialog box. Figure 6.9 shows the color mask.

Figure 6.9 – *Color mask for the primary image.*

The layers that contained these images were made visible and saved as a copy in the bitmap (.bmp) format, creating the primary image. The primary composited image will be used by the **backgroundImage** attribute of the **VIEW** element.

Mapping image example

A mapping image is needed to determine when and where a skin is clicked and what action should be taken. The mapping image, shown in Figure 6.10, was created with a red area and a green area.

Figure 6.10 – *Mapping image.*

The green area will be used to identify the area on the skin that will start Windows Media Player, and the red area will be used to stop it. The mapping image is the same size and shape as the primary image.

The mapping image was created by copying the button layer to a new layer and turning off the bevel and emboss effect. Flat images are needed for mapping because Windows Media Player will be looking for single color values in each area. It can only search for a color you define, for instance pure red (#FF0000), and if your image has a bevel or other effect, not all of it will be the exact red you need. To make the mapping buttons an easy color to remember, the images were filled with pure red and pure green, but any color can be used. You will need to remember the color numbers in your map so that they can be entered in the XML skin definition file. In this case, red is #FF0000 and green is #00FF00.

Then, with only the new layer visible, the image was saved as a copy to a bitmap (.bmp) file. It will be called by the **mappingImage** attribute of the **BUTTONGROUP element**.

Alternate image example

Alternate images are not required but are very useful to give visual cues to the user. In this case, a hover image is recommended so that the user knows what areas can be clicked.

An alternate image, shown in Figure 6.11, was created with two yellow buttons.

Figure 6.11 – *Alternate image.*

The alternate image was created by copying the original button layer to a new layer and then changing the fill color to yellow. The bevel and emboss effect was kept. Then a new layer was created and images were added: the arrow indicates "play" and the square indicates "stop". Then, with only the new yellow button and type layers visible, the image was saved as a copy to a bitmap file.

The result is that when the mouse hovers over an area defined by the mapping image, the hover image will be displayed, alerting users that if they click that spot, Windows Media Player will play or stop.

Final image example

Figure 6.12 shows the final image of the skin:

Figure 6.12 – *Final skin image.*

Figure 6.13 shows the image you will see if you hover over the pink button on the right.

Figure 6.13 – *Final image with the mouse hovering over the right button.*

And finally, Figure 6.14 shows the image you will see if you hover over the pink button on the left.

Figure 6.14 – *Final image with mouse hovering over the left button.*

XML code for the art example

The details of writing XML code are given in Chapter 8, but the code for the artwork in this example is shown here to demonstrate how little code is needed to create a working skin. Predefined buttons are used for the play and stop functions.

To use this simple skin, you must load a file or playlist from the Windows Media Player *anchor*. When Windows Media Player shifts to compact mode, a small box appears in the lower right corner of the screen. This box is called the anchor, and clicking it gives you the minimum functionality needed, in case a skin does not provide a way to return to full mode. The user can switch between modes by using the **View** menu while in full mode or the anchor while in compact mode.

Here is the code for the simple example skin:

```
<THEME>
  <VIEW
    clippingColor  =  "#CCCC00"
    backgroundImage  =  "background.bmp"
    titleBar  =  "false">

    <BUTTONGROUP
      mappingImage  =  "map.bmp"
      hoverImage  =  "hover.bmp">

      <PLAYELEMENT
        mappingColor  =  "#00FF00"/>

      <STOPELEMENT
        mappingColor  =  "#FF0000"/>

    </BUTTONGROUP>
  </VIEW>
</THEME>
```

CHAPTER 7

How to Design Skins

This chapter covers the theory and process of designing skins. There are several different ways to design your own original skins, but you may want to study the design process other people have used. This chapter will break that process down into four basic steps. The next chapter will use these steps to take you through the complete procedure of creating a sample skin.

User interface guidelines

There are a lot of user interface elements to choose from, but specific ones work best in specific situations. This chapter will discuss what works best where.

Most people will want to create skin art with a wide range of unique creative elements. But in some cases, people may want to create skins that look like standard Windows program user interfaces.

Windows interface

If you want to make your skin look and operate like other Windows programs, your skin might look like the Classic skin design in Figure 7.1. This skin follows the rules set forth in the Windows user interface guidelines, which is a recommended set of design principles to follow if you are creating programs for Windows. If you'd like to know more about designing standard user interfaces for Windows applications, consult the *Windows Interface Design Guide* published by Microsoft Press.

Figure 7.1 – *The Classic skin.*

The Classic skin has the standard features of a Windows user interface, which are:

Title bar
The title bar is the bar at the top of every standard window that displays the name of the window. Click and drag on the title bar to move your window around. Double-click it to maximize or restore the window.

Window button
The **Window** button is at the top left corner and shows a miniature Windows Media Player icon. Use this to restore, move, size, minimize, maximize, or close the Player.

Minimize, Maximize/Restore, Close buttons
These three buttons are at the top right and let you quickly do the most common tasks a Windows program needs.

Menus
Below the title bar are the menus. From left to right they are: **File, View, Play, Tools,** and **Help**. All Windows programs should have **File, View,** and **Help**.

For more information about how to use the user interface in Windows, see Help for Windows.

Windows Media Player interface

It's not necessary to follow the Windows user interface guidelines when creating skins. Some people may want this classic design, but most skins won't follow them because the whole point of skins is to be creative and original. Productivity applications like Microsoft Word follow the Windows user interface guidelines because users depend on a standard interface that makes it easy to learn new tasks. But most skin users want skins to be different from other programs. They don't expect a standard interface. They want something interesting and entertaining. For this reason, there are few absolute requirements for a skin interface. However, there are recommended guidelines on what will work best where.

Return to Full Mode button

There is one design element that every skin should have. Skins can only use the basic functionality of Windows Media Player, but cannot use the advanced functionality of the **Media Guide**, **Media Library**, **CD Audio**, and other features. So it's necessary to include the **Return to Full Mode** button in every skin design so that the user can return to the full mode of the Player if they want to use these advanced features.

A typical **Return to Full Mode** button looks like Figure 7.2.

Figure 7.2 – *Return to Full Mode button.*

You don't have to use the exact same artwork as Figure 7.2. Any similar design will get the idea across to the user. The reason you want to have this button is that it is possible for users to remove the anchor window. Without the anchor, there's no easy way to return to full mode, select another skin, open a new file, open a URL, or exit the Player. Whenever you start Windows Media Player, the anchor, shown in Figure 7.3, is displayed at the lower right corner of your computer screen.

Figure 7.3 – *The anchor window.*

No other user interface elements are absolutely required, but you'd have a pretty boring skin without a few other controls. The more you think about how people will use your skin, the more successful your skin will be.

Recommended controls

User interface elements that appear on the screen are called controls. There are several types of controls you can add. The following control categories will help you plan the user interface for your skin. Example code for many of these controls will be given in Chapter 9.

Minimum controls

Although the **Return to Full Mode** button may be the most important control to remember and the easiest to forget, no skin would be very useful without having the following controls.

Play

If you don't have a way to let the user start the Player playing, there isn't much point in doing a skin at all. You could have a skin that automatically started playing, but most users like to have some choice over when they begin listening or viewing.

Stop

If you've ever used a new piece of software and been frustrated because you didn't know how to turn it off, you won't want to torture your skin user with a runaway song. Providing a way to stop the Player is definitely recommended.

Playlist

By adding a playlist, you will let your users choose what they listen to and when. The playlist can be displayed on the surface of your skin or in a separate drawer or window that appears only when the user wants to look at it.

You could stop there and you'd have a minimal skin, but there's a lot more you can do to add interest to your design.

Transport controls

Transport controls are universally used in the entertainment industry for tape and CD players, VCRs, and so on. They include buttons such as **Play** and **Stop**, and their purpose is to move the audio and video. Your user will be familiar with them and you will probably want to add some or all of them.

Pause

Pause is very useful for the Player. If you just want to stop something for a moment and go back to the same place in the song or video, use **Pause.** The difference between **Pause** and **Stop** is that **Stop** doesn't just stop the Player, it rewinds the music or video to the beginning. **Pause** does not rewind.

Play/Pause

Many skins use a combined button that toggles between **Play** and **Pause**. When you click it, the Player starts playing and the button image changes to **Pause**. Click it again, the Player pauses, and the image changes to **Play**. The full mode of the Player works like this, so your user will recognize it.

Next

Your users are likely to be using playlists. Having a **Next** button to move to the next item in the playlist is very handy and definitely recommended.

Previous

Use a **Previous** button to give the user a chance to move backward in the playlist sequence.

Repeat

Some people like to listen to the same playlist over and over. You can make this easy for them by giving them a **Repeat** button.

Fast Forward

You can also add a **Fast Forward** button to let the user speed forward within a particular video. This is useful if you want to skip over something you don't like.

Fast Rewind

This is the same as **Fast Forward** except that it goes backward.

Simple sound controls

When your users are playing music or watching videos, they will want to be able to control the volume. You can make this possible in two ways.

Volume

A volume control will let the user adjust the volume in small increments. You can create volume controls by using sliders, custom sliders, or even a bunch of small buttons.

Mute

Sometimes your user will want to turn off the sound momentarily and go back to the same volume setting soon afterward. Providing a **Mute** button will make this easy.

Seek controls

Songs and videos usually start at the beginning and play until the end. But if you want to let the user move quickly through the song to a specific point, you have a few options. The ability to shift to a different part of the song and play from there is called *seeking*. Using the **Fast Forward** and **Fast Rewind** transport controls is one way to provide seeking, but there are two others.

Seek Bar

You can provide a slider, a custom slider, or a series of buttons to seek to a specific part of the song or video. By allowing users to visually choose the part of the content they want to play, you give them a very easy way to move through the program.

Markers

If you know your music or video will have markers, you can provide a series of buttons to move to specific markers. Markers can be embedded in songs or videos at specific locations and used to navigate to specific points in the content. You can learn more about markers in Chapter 12.

Windows controls

Every skin is a Windows program and is displayed in a window. The window may be hidden, but it is there. You can add the following controls to your skin to operate the basic Windows functions of your skin.

Minimize

By adding a **Minimize** button to your skin, you make it easy for the user to quickly move the skin off the desktop and put it in the Windows task bar.

Exit

If you put an **Exit** button on your skin, the user can easily quit the Player and go do something else.

Small/Restore

You can add buttons to change to fixed window sizes by using different views. For example, you could have a normal-sized skin in one view and a smaller skin in another. You could use buttons to switch back and forth. You can have as many views as is practical.

Title Bar

You can add a title bar if you want to include all of the Player's functionality. Doing so gives your user complete control over the window, but it takes away some of the visual freedom of skin design.

Most of the time you won't want to use the title bar. A title bar will add a visible rectangular edge to your skin and not allow you to take advantage of irregular shapes.

Figure 7.4 – *A skin without a title bar.*

By changing one line in the code for the skin in Figure 7.4 from

```
titleBar = "False"
```

to

```
titleBar = "True"
```

you add a title bar and window edges. Figure 7.5 shows the same skin with a title bar and window edges.

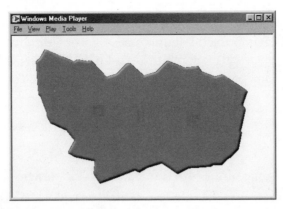

Figure 7.5 – *The same skin with a title bar and window edges.*

By setting the **titleBar** attribute to True, you provide full Player functionality. But your skin does not look as good by contemporary design standards.

However, if you want to create a purely functional skin that takes advantage of the title bar, you could use a skin like Figure 7.6, which doesn't lose anything by adding a title bar. Because the skin is designed to be purely functional and uses text boxes for all the user interface elements, the rectangular edge that comes with the title bar doesn't seem out of place.

Figure 7.6 – *A skin that uses text boxes and a title bar.*

Video controls

Unless you know that your user will never want to use your skin to play a video, you will want to add the following two controls to your skin.

Video Screen

In order to play a video, you will need to provide a place to display video on your skin. If you do not have a **VIDEO** element defined, the Player will return to the full mode to play the video, and your skin will not be used. If you don't want to display the video in the main view of your skin, you can create a sliding drawer that opens when a video starts playing. You can also use masks to create non-rectangular video windows.

Show/Hide Settings

You can provide a button to toggle back and forth between showing and hiding the settings for video, such as brightness, contrast, hue, and saturation. Because the user will only use these once in a while, you should probably put these in a separate view and display that view as a drawer or separate window.

Visualizations

If you want to give your users the ability to watch and change visualizations, add the following controls to your skin.

Visualization Screen

If you don't provide a place to show visualizations on your skin, they won't be shown. Your skin will still play music, but it will be more interesting if you let the user watch visualizations. Visualizations can use the same area of the skin as the video window. You can also display visualizations in a separate drawer or window; using masks lets you display a visualization in a non-rectangular area.

Next/Previous Visualization

If you want to give the user the ability to change the current visualization, you should provide buttons that display the next and previous visualization.

Visualization Name and Preset Text

If you provide buttons to change the visualization, you should also provide a way to display the visualization name and preset name through a **TEXT** element.

Advanced sound controls

You can also provide the user with the ability to change the way the sound is reproduced by the Player. Consider the following possible additions, which could be combined with the simpler sound settings such as **Volume** and **Mute**.

Equalizer settings

You can display an equalizer to adjust the 10 bands of frequency that the Player can control. Using sliders for each band, you can let the user boost the bass and tweak the treble. You can provide this ability through a separate window or drawer. You can also provide extra buttons to display and control the equalizer presets, such as "Rock", "Rap", and so on.

Stereo settings

You can let the user adjust the stereo balance of the sound by using sliders. This can be part of the same window or drawer as the equalizer, or it can be done separately.

Help control

If your skin is complicated enough, you might want to create a Help file that is displayed when a user clicks a button. This can also contain your name and e-mail address so people can send you feedback.

A process for designing skins

There are as many ways to create something original as there are things to be created. Each skin you create may be done differently, but this section gives you a step-by-step procedure you can follow to put all the pieces together to create your own original skins. In Chapter 8 you will use these steps to create a sample skin that will help you learn the whole process.

Here are the four steps:

Step 1: Analyze what to do

Decide what you want your user to do. What functions do you want to provide? You can do this in your head or on paper, but the important thing is to be aware of what you want the user of your skin to be able to do. For example, you will want to examine what can be done to control the media, such as starting, stopping, and so on.

Step 2. Design the user interface

Sketch out your user interface. Decide which buttons, text, windows, and sliders you want to provide to users so they can control the functions you chose in step 1. You may want to draw your ideas on paper to see how they fit into the image size you will be working with.

Step 3. Create the art

Get the art program of your choice and make the art files you want the user to see. As you read in Chapter 6, you will need three types of art files: background images, secondary images, and mapping images.

Step 4. Write the code

Write the skin definition file that will link everything together with XML and JScript. You may need to create extra JScript files if your code gets complicated.

Step 1: Analyzing what to do

The most important part of any journey is deciding where you want to go. When you are approaching something new, like skin design, it may seem like a confusing mess of things to decide. It's easiest to break down the steps into simple tasks so that you can concentrate on one thing at a time.

The first step in skin design is figuring out what you want the skin to do. This might sound obvious, but it's important to decide what user interface elements you will use first. Later, you can figure out how the skin will look and what the code will consist of.

Start by asking yourself what you want from a Player and then see if it can be done. Study other players and other kinds of equipment such as television sets for ideas. You must decide what you want the Player to do when your skin is being used. Do you want to give the user a **Mute** button or a **Repeat** button?

Don't worry about what you think the Player is capable of doing at this point, just think about what you'd like it to do. The possibilities are far greater than you may think.

Your analysis doesn't need to take a long time, but you want to come away from this step with a list. For example, you could make a list of Player functions that would look like this:

- Play
- Stop
- Return to Full Mode
- Volume

By making a list, it's much easier to plan for things before you create them than to try to add them after you've done a lot of work. If you've worked hard creating a beautiful piece of art, you don't want to have to redo it because you forgot to include a **Stop** button.

Of course the design process is never this simple, and your art and coding tools will let you make lots of changes easily. But a small plan now will save you lots of time later.

At this point, you might want to take a little break and do something else. Give your mind a bit of time to absorb the things you want to accomplish with your skin. Then try going back to your list, and see if there is something you may have forgotten.

For more ideas on what the Player can do, see the Windows Media Player 7 SDK, which is on the companion CD.

Step 2: Designing the user interface

Now that you've decided what you want the Player to do, the second step is to decide how the user will make this happen. You still don't want to think about artwork or coding at this point. Resist any temptation to start using Photoshop or typing XML. Think of what users can do with the Player. They can click with a mouse and press keys on the keyboard. That's all. But that's a great deal. Look at your list from step 1 and ask yourself, "How can the user make this happen?"

For example, if you want to give the user the ability to change the volume, think of how that might be accomplished. You could do it with a simple slider; you could do it with a unique custom slider that looks like a stalk of corn; you could do it with a series of buttons. There are hundreds of ways to do it. You may want to look at other skins and other types of software for ideas. You may be inspired by anything in the world around you. Make notes and sketches that you can refer to later.

Here is a list of possible user interface elements:

- Buttons
- Sliders
- Progress bars
- Custom sliders
- Text controls
- Video display window

- Visualization display window

- Playlist display window

- Separate windows

- Hidden drawers

- Sliding drawers

After you've made your final sketch, take that sketch and compare it to the list of functions that you made in step 1. Be sure that the items on this list correspond to the items in the sketch of design elements that you made in step 2.

Step 3: Creating the art

Now you can take your sketch and turn it into finished art. Even if you're not a professional artist, you can still do amazing things with computer art programs such as Photoshop, Paint Shop Pro, or Jedor, Inc.Viscosity. Using an art program makes it relatively easy to create simple art because you can start with basic shapes and modify them until you're done.

As you saw in Chapter 6, there are three kinds of art you must create:

Primary image
You only need to make one file for the primary image. This will contain the basic shape of your skin, as well as the masking color outside your shape. This will also contain whatever surface details you want the user to see on your skin.

Mapping images
If you are using the button groups, you will want to create a mapping image. This will not be seen by the user but will serve as a way to tell the Player what to do when a particular region of your skin is clicked by the user.

Alternate images
You will want to give users visual cues when they click parts of your skin. You might want to have one image appear when the user hovers over a button and another when the user clicks the button. Your alternate image will appear when a particular event happens (such as hovering or clicking).

Basic procedure to create your art

The art creation process assumes you are using a computer program like Adobe Photoshop which has layers. If you are using an art program that doesn't have layers, you will need to follow a slightly different procedure. The companion CD has an article on a process to create skins without using layers.

Chapter 8 will go into more detail about these procedures, where you will create a sample skin. Here are the procedures for creating your skin art:

- Get your initial sketch of your skin into the art program by scanning, tracing, or drawing freehand. Make the sketch into a layer.

- Create a new layer and draw your basic skin shape over the sketch. In essence you're using the new layer as tracing paper over the sketch. Fill in the area around your skin shape with a masking color that is similar to the color of the edges of your skin to avoid jagged aliasing.

- When you're finished with your skin shape, create a new layer for all the buttons you want to use. Turn off the basic skin shape layer and use your sketch as a guide for drawing each button. Using layers like tracing paper over the initial sketch makes it easy to turn your sketch into finished art-work.

- After you've created your button layer, copy it as many times as you have alternate images. Copy it again for your mapping image.

- Now that you've made copies of your original button layer, hide all the layers you copied the buttons to. Then merge the visible layers together. You should see an image that contains your basic skin shape, the buttons you want the user to see, and the masking color outside your shape. Save the merged layer as a bitmap and name it something like "background.bmp". Write down the number for the masking color so you can remember it later. It should be a six-digit hexadecimal number preceeded by a number sign (#).

- Hide the background layer that you just saved. Now, one at a time, unhide the other button layers. Redraw or color each one to create the image you want to show for each alternate button image. For example, if your normal buttons were green, you might want a yellow layer to indicate hovering and red layer to indicate that a mouse button was clicked. As you finish the layer for each alternate image, give it a name you can remember, save it as a bitmap, and then hide the layer.

- When you've created all your alternate images, you should have one layer left. This is your mapping image. For this you want pure colors. If your buttons have texture (that is, you've created button areas with mixed colors), smooth out the texture so that only one color remains for each button area. Then fill each button with a completely different color and write down those color numbers. Save the mapping image as a bitmap, give it a name like "map.bmp" and hide the layer.

- You should now see nothing in your art program, but you've created all the pieces of art and saved them as separate files. Save the master file of your art program and close it. You've created a set of art files for a skin.

You can vary this process widely as you get more familiar with a particular art program. Often you will want to create many layers, breaking all the pieces of the art down into manageable components.

Step 4: Writing the code

Now that you've created the art, writing the code is next. You know what you want the Player to do. You know what the user interface should do. You've created the artwork for the user interface. Now it's time to tie it all together with a skin definition file.

Look at your user interface sketch and your list of actions that you want the Player to do from your skin. For every action, you must have a line of code that tells the Player what to do. You will trigger these actions by having the user click a button. Each button must have an element that defines it.

Basic procedure to create your code

The first step in coding is to create your skin definition file. Open a new file and give it a name with the file name extension .wms. Here is the basic process for creating your code. Chapter 8 will go into more detail on each step when you create the sample skin featured in that chapter.

- Create your **THEME** element first. You've only got one. <THEME> should be the first line of your code and </THEME> should be the last.

- Create your **VIEW** elements next. Usually you'll only have one when you're starting out, but you can create more than one theme. Indent each set of elements a small amount so you can keep track of closing tags and levels of coding structure.

- Define the attributes for each **THEME** element.

- Create any "enclosing" elements next. For example, the **BUTTONGROUP** element will include at least two **BUTTONELEMENT** elements. First create the **BUTTONGROUP** elements and define any attributes.

- Then create the elements that will be enclosed. If you have a **BUTTONGROUP**, you'll need to create **BUTTONELEMENT** elements nested inside it. Assign attributes to each button.

- Create any other elements that you need and assign them attributes.

- After you have created your user interface with XML elements, the next step is to write JScript code that triggers actions in the Player when the user clicks various parts of your skin.

- You can also create event handlers that will modify your skin when something happens inside the Player; for example, you can write code that tells the Player what to do when the song ends.

As you design your code, think of the Player as one person and your user as another. Your art is the window that lets the two people see each other, but the code is the way that they can actually talk to each other. The user can talk to the Player and the Player can talk to the user, but only by using your art and your code.

Think of the XML elements as the scaffolding that holds your artwork up and the code as the wiring that connects your artwork to the Player.

Here is an example that creates a simple skin. The first thing that you do is to create the **THEME** and **VIEW** elements.

```
<THEME>
   <VIEW
      clippingColor  =   "#CCCC00"
      backgroundImage  =   "background.bmp"
      titleBar = "false">

   </VIEW>
</THEME>
```

This code sets up the skin with a **THEME** element and one **VIEW** element. The **VIEW** element defines the clipping color, background image, and title bar values. It will be easier to edit your code if you indent each pair of nested elements as shown.

After you've created your basic skin shell, add the code for the **BUTTONGROUP** element. Your file will now look like this:

```
<THEME>
    <VIEW
        clippingColor   =   "#CCCC00"
        backgroundImage   =   "background.bmp"
        titleBar   =   "false">

        <BUTTONGROUP
            mappingImage   =   "map.bmp"
            hoverImage   =   "hover.bmp"
            downImage   =   "down.bmp">

        </BUTTONGROUP>
    </VIEW>
</THEME>
```

The new code you added is in bold. It sets up a **BUTTONGROUP** set of elements and defines the mapping image, the hover image, and the down image.

Finally, add the code for each **BUTTONELEMENT** in the **BUTTONGROUP**. The finished code will look like this:

```
<THEME>
    <VIEW
        clippingColor   =   "#CCCC00"
        backgroundImage   =   "background.bmp"
        titleBar   =   "false"   >

        <BUTTONGROUP
            mappingImage   =   "map.bmp"
            hoverImage   =   "hover.bmp"
            downImage   =   "down.bmp">

            <BUTTONELEMENT
                upToolTip   =   "Open  and  play  the  file  'laure.wma""
                onClick   =   "JScript:player.URL   =   '.\\..\\media\\laure.wma';"
                mappingColor   =   "#00FF00"   />

            <BUTTONELEMENT
```

```
            upToolTip  =  "Close"
            onClick  =  ""JScript:  view.close();""
            mappingColor  =  "#FF0000"/>


        </BUTTONGROUP>
     </VIEW>
  </THEME>
```

The new code is in bold. Each **BUTTONELEMENT** is defined with a ToolTip, a click event handler, and a mapping color. The click events load a line of JScript that takes an action. The first button loads a file into the Player and starts it playing. The second button exits the Player.

The code for this simple skin gives you a small taste of what skins can do. This chapter has focused on the guidelines for what a skin should contain. Now it is time to apply what you have learned. The next chapter will give you a step-by-step tutorial on creating a complete skin.

Creating a Sample Skin

The purpose of this chapter is to show you how to create skins using a step-by-step procedure that will produce a sample skin. No drawing skills are required, and the programming will consist of only a few lines. To make it even easier, the artwork will be uncomplicated and the sample skin will have only three controls. Your finished skin will look like Figure 8.1.

Figure 8.1 – *Sample skin with three controls.*

In this chapter, you'll create a sample skin by following the four steps that were first introduced in Chapter 7.

Step 1: Analyze what to do
Choose the functionality of your skin and decide what you want the skin to do.

Step 2: Design the user interface
Select the default visual elements that the user will see and the additional elements that will appear when specific events occur.

Step 3: Create the art
Use an art program to create art for backgrounds, buttons, textures, and so on.

Step 4: Write the code
Type the definitions and commands that the skin requires so that it can respond properly when the user takes an action.

Each of these steps will be explained in detail as you go through them to create your sample skin. You may want to refer back to Chapters 6 and 7 for more information about skin programming and design.

Step 1: Analyze what to do

The first step in creating your own skin design is to decide what the skin will do. While it may be tempting to start creating buttons and writing code, your design will be better if you plan the player functionality before you do anything else.

The best way to start is by making a list of what you want Windows Media Player to do. Remember that the purpose of a skin is to control the Player behind the skin. At this stage, don't think of exactly *how* your skin will control Windows Media Player, only of *what* you want the Player to do.

For ideas on going beyond the user interface recommendations for the sample skin featured in this chapter, see the Windows Media Player 7 SDK on the companion CD that comes with this book. The SDK includes a complete reference to all Windows Media Player functionality. For a detailed list of other Player functions, see Chapter 7. Because Windows Media Player provides a very large set of options through JScript and XML, don't limit your imagination.

Basic functionality of the sample skin

To make things easy, this sample skin will have only three controls: **Play**, **Stop**, and **Return to Full Mode**. These are the three basic functions that every skin should have; others are optional. Start a list with these three.

Making it play

The first function to plan for is the ability to start the Player playing. You could have the music play automatically when you start Windows Media Player, but most users will want to have control of the play function.

At this point, don't worry about how the play functionality will be implemented, or what the button or slider will look like; just add it to your list.

Making it stop

Next comes the ability to stop the playback. Again, how this is done isn't important, but you should never have a **Play** without a **Stop**.

Making it return to full mode

One more button should be on every skin. Providing the user with the ability to return to the full mode of Windows Media Player is very important. This allows the user to get back to the complete functionality of Windows Media Player and do things that your skin can't do. The user may want to download media files to a portable device, get new content from the Media Guide, download a new visualization, or do other tasks that can't be accomplished in a skin.

That's all you need for the basic functionality of the sample skin. Figure 8.2 shows a listing of what the Player will do in this skin.

What do I want the Player to do?

1. Make it play.

2. Make it stop.

3. Let the user return to full mode easily.

Figure 8.2 – *List of proposed Player functionality.*

Step 2: Design the user interface

Now that you have a list of what you want Windows Media Player to do, the next step is to design a user interface. Your skin is an interface between the outside world of the user and the inside world of the computer and Windows Media Player. Until a user interface is attached to the functionality of the Player, the code just sits there and does nothing. The user interface of the skin makes it possible for Windows Media Player to come to life by responding to the clicks and keystrokes of the user.

What user interface elements are available?

Windows Media Player provides several XML elements to choose from when designing an interface. When you design your own skins, you can use buttons, sliders, text controls and more. Because each element is programmable through XML and JScript, the possibilities are endless. For example, you might want to start a media clip playing with a simple button, but you could also use a **CustomSlider** element to create a knob that turns the Player on and off but is also a volume control.

In choosing your interface elements, keep your audience in mind. If you want people to be able to use your skin easily, follow the user interface recomendations given in Chapter 7. If you want to appeal to people who are willing to explore and play with your interface, go wild with your imagination.

The sample skin that will be created in this chapter will only contain the most basic user interface elements, but your own original designs can include almost anything you can imagine.

What will the sample user interface do?

Start with the functionality list in Figure 8.2. The list includes Play, Stop, and Return to Full Mode. Next, you will need to provide user interface elements for the functions on the list.

The process of designing each interface element is divided into four parts:

- Make a rough sketch of the basic shape of the skin.

- Choose the kinds of interface controls you want to have for each function.

- Add the interface controls to your sketch.

- Think about how to give clues and cues to the user with alternate images.

Sketching your basic skin shape

Skins must have a general shape and an overall size. You can make one as big as the whole screen or as small as an icon. At this point you should sit down and sketch what you want your skin's basic shape to be. You don't have to limit yourself to a single shape; for example, you could have a connected series of floating circles of different sizes.

For the sample skin that will be created in this chapter, a simple oval will be used. You can think of this as the tray that holds your user interface elements. The part inside the tray will contain the user interface controls. The part outside the tray will be transparent, letting other Windows applications and the desktop show through. Figure 8.3 shows a simple sketch of the sample skin shape.

Figure 8.3 – *Sample skin shape.*

Choosing the user interface controls

There are several interface controls to choose from, but the simplest type is a button. Each function you'll probably want to use can be triggered by a button. You will need three button designs for the functions of the sample skin: **Play**, **Stop**, and **Return to Full Mode**.

Adding the controls to your sketch

The next question to ask yourself is where you want the buttons to be located on your skin. Add these user interface controls to the sketch of your sample skin's basic shape. Figure 8.4 shows a sketch of a three-button skin.

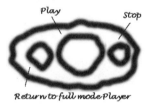

Figure 8.4 – *Three buttons in a row.*

Adding clues and cues

Now that you've decided on the basics of what you want your skin to look like, you'll want to think about ways to add alternate art that can interact with users. One way is to give users *clues* to tell them what they can do, and the other is to give them *cues* to tell them what they have done.

Clues

You should provide the user with clues to what your interface does. If you have a skin with only a few buttons on it and nothing else, the user will probably figure out what to do. But if you have a complicated drawing or use a real photograph, users may not know where to click. To solve this problem, Windows Media Player can temporarily show a different art image when the user hovers the mouse cursor over a specific area of your skin.

In this chapter, you will learn how to provide hover art that will alert users that they can click a particular button. This will use the **MouseOver** event and will be called the hover clue.

Besides a hover clue, your skin should provide a ToolTip for each button. ToolTips are small text messages that appear when you hover the cursor over a region of the skin. Usually there is a short delay before a ToolTip appears on the screen. Hover images, however, appear instantly. Using both kinds of clues will give users a good idea of what they can do with your skin.

Add a note to your sketch indicating where you want to provide art that will give hover and ToolTip clues to the user.

Cues

When a user clicks a button, something usually happens right away, but not always. Sometimes Microsoft Windows is busy and can't do everything fast enough. Sometimes the Player itself takes a few seconds to find a file and open it. In order to prevent user frustration, give users a visual cue that they can perform an action.

In this chapter you will learn how to provide a temporary image that will be displayed when the user clicks a button. This will use the **MouseDown** event and will be called the down cue.

Add a note to your sketch indicating that you want to provide art that will give a down cue to the user.

Step 3: Create the art

Now that your functionality has been chosen, and you have finished sketching your user interface design, it's time to create the art for your skin. For most skins, you will create three types of art.

Types of art

The art for skins must perform three different tasks.

- Primary images display the skin on the screen.

- Mapping images connect buttons to the Player.

- Alternate images give clues and cues to the user.

Primary images

First you must create a primary image for your skin. This is what the users will see when they install your skin. The primary image is composed of one or more images that are created by specific skin elements.

Each **VIEW** element will have a background image that you can add other element images to, allowing you to create a primary composite image. You also may have secondary images, such as a sliding tray, that are not displayed when your skin first appears, but that appear when the user takes some action. These follow the same rules as primary images, in that they are created with a set of elements.

If you have overlapping images, you must specify the *z-order*. The z-order uses a number to define which image will be displayed in front of another one. Images with higher z-orders will be displayed in front of ones with lower numbers.

Mapping images

One of the most powerful features of Windows Media Player skins is that you can use mapping images to trigger events for your skin. Mapping images are files that contain bitmap information that is not meant to be viewed by the user, but is used by Windows Media Player to take action when the user clicks somewhere on your skin. In essence, the user cannot see mapping images, but the mouse can.

Each control uses a different color for a region of the mapping image. For example, if you color part of a mapping image a specific red value, and the user clicks the corresponding area of your primary image, a button will fire an event. Color is used to define which events are triggered by clicks in specific regions of the skin. This may sound odd, but it allows a great deal of artistic control over the actions that your skin can process.

Alternate images

You can also set up alternate images to give the user clues about what they can do and cues when they do something. For example, you can create an alternate image of a button that will be displayed only when the mouse hovers over the button. This is a good way to let users know what they can do, and also makes the user interface more discoverable. By using ToolTips and hover images creatively, you can make unusual user interfaces that still give feedback on what options are available. You can also use alternate images to give visual feedback when users click a button.

Creating the primary image file

You will need to create a primary image file to contain the art that is displayed on the screen. You need to create your art file by combining the layers you created in your art program. The reason for using layers is that you can copy and modify the layers later to create mapping image files and alternate art files.

Using layers

To make the primary art file, you will need to create layers in the following order. If you don't have an art program that uses layers, there is an article on the companion CD that shows you how to create a skin without layers.

Skin background layer
> This is the color that will be transparent when the skin is displayed. Create a layer for this first, but choose the final color of this layer after you choose a color for the skin container layer. This color should be similar to, but not the same as, the skin container layer, to hide any anti-aliasing effects.

Skin container layer
> This is the image that will form the outline of your skin and will be what the user sees. It will also be the container for the three buttons in the sample skin. Think of your skin as a container for user interface controls such as buttons, sliders, and so on. In the sample, the container is an oval.

Play, Stop, and Return to Full Mode button layers

These are the three user interface controls that this sample skin uses. You can put them in separate layers so that you can easily adjust them or copy them later.

Creating the primary image with Photoshop

All instructions for creating the art are given for Adobe Photoshop, but any other art program can be used to create skins as long as you can save to one of the file formats supported by Windows Media Player (.bmp, .gif, .jpg, and .png). You will find it easier to create skins if you use an art program that has layers, such as Adobe Photoshop, Jasc Paint Shop Pro, or Jedor Viscosity. Layers are extremely useful because images must be perfectly aligned in order for mapping images and alternate images to work properly.

Before you create your layers, you must create the file that will hold your layers. Start Photoshop and create a new file that is 100 pixels high and 200 pixels wide.

Skin background layer

To create the primary image for the sample skin, the first thing you need to do is make a new layer and name it *Skin background*. This will become the transparency color you will define in the skin definition file. Wait until the color for the skin container is chosen before filling the skin background layer with a specific color.

Skin container layer

Next create another new layer and call it *Skin container*. This will define the edges of your skin and will be the container for the buttons.

Choose a foreground color for the shape, using the Web color sliders. In this example, the color #00FFFF was chosen.

Next create an oval shape. The easiest way is to use the Elliptical Marquee tool and create an oval selection. When you have created an oval selection that is the size and shape you want, fill the selection with the foreground color and deselect the selection.

Your skin container layer should look like Figure 8.5.

Figure 8.5 – *Skin container layer.*

Background skin color

Now that you have chosen a foreground color for your skin container shape, you can choose a similar color for your skin background layer. You do not want the exact same color, or your skin container will be transparent also. In fact, be sure you do not use the background color anywhere else in your skin, even in photographs, because wherever this color appears, the desktop image will show through.

You want a color similar to the skin container color to avoid anti-aliasing effects. For example, if you have a black background, some bits of black may show up around the edge of your skin. By choosing a color close to the color of the skin container, any stray pixels that show up in the anti-aliasing process will not be noticed.

Anti-aliasing is the process of smoothing the edges of slanted or curved shapes. Anti-aliasing creates new colors, for pixels along the edges of a shape, that are a blend of the foreground color and the background color. Some of these in-between colors can cause pixels to be missed when the background color is made transparent. In this case the color chosen is #33CCFF.

Your sample skin background layer should look like Figure 8.6.

Figure 8.6 – *Skin background layer.*

Stop, Play, and Return button layers

Create a new layer and name it *Stop button*. Using the Elliptical Marquee selection tool again, create a circle and position it on the left side of the overall image. Turn on the visibility of the skin container file to help place the selection.

When you are satisfied with the placement, fill the selection with a color (but don't use the color of the skin container or the skin background). Then deselect the selection and apply a Bevel and Emboss layer effect. If you want to apply non-layer effects to your button, make a copy of the original for later use in mapping.

Create a new layer and draw a square in it for the stop symbol. When the two layers are combined, your **Stop** button should look like Figure 8.7.

Figure 8.7 – *Stop button.*

Create a new layer and name it *Play button*. Use the same techniques you did for the **Stop** button. Any color can be used as long as it is not the same color as the skin container (because it would blend into the container) or the skin background color (because it would become transparent).

Create a new layer and draw a triangle in it for the play symbol. When the two layers are combined, your **Play** button should look like Figure 8.8.

Figure 8.8 – *Play button.*

Create a new layer and name it *Return button*. Use the same techniques you did for the **Stop** button. Any color can be used as long as it is not the same color as the skin container or the skin background color.

Create a new layer and draw two small squares in it as a simplified image of the symbol for returning to full mode. When the two layers are combined, your **Return** button should look like Figure 8.9.

Figure 8.9 – *Return button.*

Combine layers and save

You are now ready to create the primary art file. Hide all layers and then show only the following layers, in this order (top to bottom):

Play button

Close button

Return button

Skin container

Skin background

Save to a new file using the **Save a Copy** command from the **File** menu. Click the **BMP** option in the **Save As** portion of the **Save a Copy** dialog box, and type a file name that you will refer to later in your skin definition file. Ideally you should save this in the same directory as your skin definition file. For example, you could call this background.bmp. Choose the default settings and save the file.

Your primary art file should look like Figure 8.10.

Figure 8.10 – *Primary art file.*

You will use this file name as the value for the **backgroundImage** attribute of the **VIEW** element in your skin definition file.

Creating the mapping image

After you have created the pieces of your primary art file, it is relatively easy to create a mapping-image file. You will create the new mapping-image file by combining the art from the three button layers you already created.

1. Take the three buttons you created for the primary art file and copy them to a new layer. Use the following steps: Copy the Stop button layer, remove any Layer effects, and rename it *Stop map*. The art should look flat, with no bevels.

2. Use the Color Picker to create a foreground color of pure red. Be sure the color number value is #FF0000. Then use the Paint Bucket tool to fill the inside of the circle of the Stop map layer.

3. Copy the Play button layer, remove any Layer effects, and rename it *Play map*. Again, the art should look flat. You do not want any effects in the mapping layer because you are just defining regions of the bitmap that Windows Media Player will use to determine where the mouse performs an action and what you want to do about the action.

4. Use the Color Picker to create a foreground color of pure green. Be sure the color number value is #00FF00. Then use the Paint Bucket tool to fill the inside of the circle of the Play map layer.

5. Use the same process to create the mapping image for the **Return** button. Blue will be used, with a value of #0000FF

You are now ready to create the mapping image file. Hide all layers, and then show only the following layers, in this order (top to bottom):

Play map

Close map

Return map

Save to a new file using the **Save a Copy** command from the **File** menu. Click the **BMP** option in the **Save As** portion of the **Save a Copy** dialog box, and type a file name that you will refer to later in your skin definition file. Ideally it should be in the same directory as your skin definition file. For example, you could call this file map.bmp. Choose the default settings and save the file.

Your mapping image should look like Figure 8.11.

Figure 8.11 – *Mapping image.*

As you might guess, the green area will be used to determine when to make Windows Media Player start, and the red area is for telling it to stop. Any two colors can be used, as long as you use their color numbers when you set up the skin definition file. Be sure the colors in the map are pure colors for the region you want to use and have distinct edges. A pure color is one where every single pixel in the area has the same color value. Using an effect may blur or distort the edge, thereby slightly modifying the colors of some of the pixels.

The mapping file is only used by the mouse, and is never seen by a user, so do not bother decorating it. Also, remove any layer effects you may have carried over from other layers.

When you save your file, the file name you choose will later be used as the value for the **mappingImage** attribute of the **BUTTONGROUP** element in your skin definition file.

Creating the hover image

The primary image of this skin is three buttons sitting on an oval. To give the user a clue about what to do, you can add hover images. These are alternate images that are displayed when the user hovers a mouse over a button. The hover buttons will also contain the play and stop VCR control symbols, as well as a simplified symbol for returning to full mode, so that users will know exactly what they can do. Using hover images allows you to create complex, self-documenting, artistic skins.

To create the hover image, you will need to take the three buttons you created for the primary art file, copy them to new layers, and add further layers for the text. Use the following steps:

1. Copy the Stop button layer and rename it *Stop hover*. Do the same with the Stop symbol layer.

2. Use the Color Picker to create a light blue foreground color (#66FFFF). This was chosen to contrast with the button colors. Then use the Paint Bucket tool to fill the inside of the circle in the Stop hover layer.

3. Copy the Play button layer and rename it *Play hover*. Do the same with the Play symbol layer.

4. Use the Paint Bucket tool to fill the inside of the circle in the Play hover layer with the same color as the Stop hover circle.

5. Follow the same steps for the **Return** button and symbol.

You are now ready to create the hover art file. Hide all layers, and then show only the following layers, in this order (top to bottom):

Play symbol hover

Stop symbol hover

Return symbol hover

Play button hover

Stop button hover

Return button hover

Save to a new file using the **Save a Copy** command from the **File** menu. Click the **BMP** option in the **Save As** portion of the **Save a Copy** dialog box, and type a file name that you will refer to later in your skin definition file. Ideally you should save this in the same directory as your skin definition file. For example, you could call this hover.bmp. Choose the default settings and save the file.

Your hover art file should look like Figure 8.12.

Figure 8.12 – *Hover art file.*

Each hover button will appear in place of the corresponding normal button when the mouse hovers over that button. If you hover over the center button in your skin, the lighter-colored **Play** button will appear, and if you hover over the right button, the user will see the lighter-colored **Stop** button. You will never see more than one hover image at a time, because the mouse cannot hover over more than one button at a time.

When you save your file, the file name you choose will later be used as the value for the **hoverImage** attribute of the **BUTTONGROUP** element in your skin definition file.

Creating the down image

The primary image of this skin is three buttons sitting on an oval. To give the user a cue about what has happened, you can add down images. These are alternate images that are displayed when the user clicks a button. The down buttons will also contain the play, stop, and return control symbols so that users will know exactly what they can do. Using down images allows you to provide visual feedback to the user.

To create the down image, you will need to follow the same steps you used to create the hover image. In essence, take the three buttons you created for the primary art file, copy them to new layers, and recolor them. In this example, the color #FF00FF was used. Your final layer should be called *Down image* and your file should be called down.bmp.

Your down art file should look like Figure 8.13.

Figure 8.13 – *Down art file.*

Each purple down button will appear in place of the corresponding normal button when the user clicks that button. If you click the middle button in your skin, the **Play** button will turn purple, and if you click the right button, the **Stop** button will turn purple.

When you save your file, the file name you choose will later be used as the value for the **downImage** attribute of the **BUTTONGROUP** element in your skin definition file.

Step 4: Write the code

Now you're ready to write the code that will tell Windows Media Player what to do for each user interface element in your skin. To do this, you must create the skin definition file that will contain all the XML elements and inline JScript code.

Creating the skin definition file

The skin definition file is a simple text file. You can create skin definition files in any text editor that saves ASCII plain text files, such as Microsoft Notepad, Microsoft Visual InterDev, or Microsoft Visual Studio. Because you will be writing XML, not HTML, you may not want to use an HTML editor; it may add extra codes you do not want or may tell you about errors that you do not have. You will probably want to avoid word processors such as Microsoft Word; even though Word can save plain text files, you may not want to have to remember to **Save As** text every time you save.

Using XML structure

The skin definition file is written in XML. One of the important features of XML is that it is completely structured, and is similar to an outline. The XML code is simply a series of elements such as **VIEW** and **BUTTONGROUP**. You will start with the elements and then define them with attributes. The rest of this tutorial will give you details on the attributes, but here is the outline of the elements that will be used:

```
<THEME>
    <VIEW>
        <BUTTONGROUP>
            <BUTTONELEMENT/>
            <BUTTONELEMENT/>
            <BUTTONELEMENT/>
        </BUTTONGROUP>
    </VIEW>
</THEME>
```

By keeping in mind the simple structure of the elements, you can make sense of the attributes that make each element unique. Details of each element will be covered in the remaining topics of this section. For more information about elements and attributes, see the Windows Media Player 7 SDK.

Starting with THEME and VIEW

Every skin must have exactly one **THEME** element and at least one **VIEW** element.

Using your text editor, create the following text:

```
<THEME>
    <VIEW
        clippingColor   =   "#33CCFF"
        backgroundImage  =   "simpskin.bmp"
        titleBar = "false">
    </VIEW>
</THEME>
```

Leave some blank lines before the closing **VIEW** tag because you'll be adding more code here later.

Save your file with any file name you wish, but be sure that the extension is .wms. For example, a typical file name might be simpskin.wms.

Every skin must start with <THEME> and end with </THEME>. You must have one and only one **THEME** element in your skin.

You must also have at least one **VIEW** element. You can have more than one **VIEW**, but this example only has one. You must have an opening <VIEW> tag and a closing </VIEW> tag. Notice that the opening <VIEW> tag does not end the tag right away, but includes several attributes before the closing angle bracket (>). The following attributes are used in the **THEME** element in this example:

clippingColor

> You will not always need the **clippingColor** attribute if the edges of your skin are rectangular. The skin in this example is oval-shaped, so you need a clipping color for the parts of the skin that you want to see the desktop through; essentially all parts that are outside the oval. In this example skin, we will use an aqua color (#33CCFF). Essentially, this value will always be a number that you get from your art program.

backgroundImage

> This is the name of the primary art file. It should be the exact file name of your primary art file. Only .bmp, .jpg, .gif, and .png files are supported, and .bmp is recommended. All the art files should be included in the .wmz file.

titleBar

> This skin does not have a **titleBar**, so the value will be "false". You only want a title bar if you want your skin to have a background color and be rectangular.

Be sure that you put the closing angle bracket (>) after the **titleBar** value to indicate that you are finished defining the **VIEW element**. Leave a few blank lines before the closing VIEW and THEME tags. You will need the lines for code that you add later.

Adding the BUTTONGROUP

This example uses the **BUTTONGROUP** element for the coding in the skin definition file. **BUTTONGROUP** creates an easy way to process mouse events without having to calculate exact locations on the screen, and it uses color for positioning instead of x-coordinates and y-coordinates.

First you must add the **BUTTONGROUP** tags to the skin definition file you created. Put them after the **VIEW** tag attributes. Leave a few blank lines inside the **BUTTONGROUP** element for the buttons you will add next.

```
<BUTTONGROUP
    mappingImage  =  "map.bmp"
    hoverImage    =  "hover.bmp"
    downImage     =  "down.bmp">



</BUTTONGROUP>
```

The following attributes are used to define the **BUTTONGROUP element**:

mappingImage

This is the file name of the mapping image file you created before, the one with the red and green circles. This attribute is required for any **BUTTONGROUP**.

hoverImage

This is the file name of the hover art file you created before, the one with the three light blue buttons for **Play** and **Stop** and **Return**. This is not required, but a hover image helps to provide clue-type feedback to the user.

downImage

This is the file name of the down art file you created before, the one with the three purple buttons for **Play** and **Stop** and **Return**. This is not required, but a down image helps to provide cue-type feedback to the user.

Adding the Play BUTTONELEMENT

Finally, you can add the **BUTTONELEMENT** elements that connect the visual buttons on the screen to Windows Media Player actions. This is the core of your skin and you can think of it as wiring the surface of the skin to the inner machinery of Windows Media Player.

BUTTONELEMENT elements are contained within a **BUTTONGROUP**. You must always have at least one **BUTTONELEMENT** inside each **BUTTONGROUP**.

Put the code for the Play **BUTTONELEMENT** after the closing angle bracket at the end of the **BUTTONGROUP attributes**.

```
<BUTTONELEMENT
    mappingColor  =  "#00FF00"
    onClick  =  "JScript:  player.URL='file:laure.wma';"
    upToolTip  =  "Play"  />
```

The following attributes are used to define the **BUTTONELEMENT** for the **Play** button:

mappingColor

This is the color value of a region in the mapping art file you created before. In this case it is the solid green color. This attribute is required for any **BUTTONELEMENT**. By defining this color, you are telling Windows Media Player to associate this color area with the XML code of this button.

onClick

This defines the event that occurs when the user clicks the button. The value of this event attribute is called an event handler and will be either a line of Microsoft JScript code, or a JScript function in an external text file that is loaded by the **loadScript** attribute of a **VIEW element**. In this case, the JScript code calls the **URL** property of Windows Media Player, which loads and starts playing a file named laure.wma. The line ends with a semicolon inside the quotes, which is good JScript coding practice. Note the use of single quotes inside the double quotes to set off the file name. For more information about JScript, see the Windows Media Player 7 SDK.

upToolTip

This defines the text that will be displayed if the user hovers the mouse over the button. Do not confuse this with the hover art that will be displayed. A ToolTip is a small balloon caption that takes a moment to appear. The hover art image, however, will appear instantly in whatever color and shape you choose.

Notice that there is no ending **BUTTONELEMENT** tag. If an element does not enclose another element, you can close it off with the forward slash just before the closing angle bracket. This tells XML that you are finished with that element. For example,

```
<BUTTONELEMENT>    </BUTTONELEMENT>
```

and

```
<BUTTONELEMENT/>
```

convey the same information in XML.

The power of skins comes from using event handlers. If the user does something with a mouse, you can handle that event with JScript. Your code can be a single line that makes Windows Media Player do something simple like play, or it can be a complete application written in JScript.

Adding the Stop BUTTONELEMENT

The **Stop** button is similar in concept to the **Play** button, but has different codes and colors.

Put the code for the Stop **BUTTONELEMENT** after the closing angle bracket of the Play **BUTTONELEMENT**.

```
<BUTTONELEMENT
    mappingColor  =  "#FF0000"
    onClick  =  "JScript:  player.controls.stop();"
    upToolTip  =  "Stop"  />
```

The following attributes are used to define the **BUTTONELEMENT** for the **Stop** button:

mappingColor

This is the color value of the region in the mapping image file you created. In this case it is the solid red color. This attribute is required for any **BUTTONELEMENT**. By defining this color, you are telling Windows Media Player to associate this color area with the XML code of this button.

onClick

This defines the event that occurs when the user clicks the button. The value of this event attribute is called an event handler and will be either a line of Microsoft JScript code, or a JScript function in an external text file that is loaded by the **loadScript** attribute of a **VIEW element**. In this case, the JScript code calls the **stop** method of the **Controls** object, which is accessed through the **controls** property of the **Player** object, which stops Windows Media Player.

upToolTip

This defines the text that will be displayed when the user hovers the mouse over the button.

Adding the Return BUTTONELEMENT

The **Return** button is similar in concept to the **Play** button, but has different codes and colors.

Put the Return **BUTTONELEMENT** code after the closing angle bracket of the Stop **BUTTONELEMENT**.

```
<BUTTONELEMENT
    mappingColor = "#0000FF"
    onClick = "JScript: view.returnToMediaCenter();"
    upToolTip = "Return to Full Mode" />
```

The following attributes are used to define the **BUTTONELEMENT** for the **Return** button:

mappingColor

This is the color value of the region in the mapping image file you created. In this case it is the solid blue color. This attribute is required for any **BUTTONELEMENT**. By defining this color, you are telling Windows Media Player to associate this color area with the XML code of this button.

onClick

This defines the event that occurs when the user clicks the button. The value of this event attribute is called an event handler and will be either a line of Microsoft JScript code, or a JScript function in an external text file that is loaded by the **loadScript** attribute of a **VIEW element**. In this case, the JScript code calls the **returnToMediaCenter** method of the **VIEW** element, which returns Windows Media Player to the full mode view.

upToolTip

This defines the text that will be displayed when the user hovers the mouse over the button.

Complete code for sample skin

Here is the complete code for the sample skin:

```
<!-- SAMPLE SKIN -->
<THEME>
    <VIEW
        clippingColor   =   "#33CCFF"
        backgroundImage   =   "simpskin.bmp"
        titleBar   =   "false">

        <BUTTONGROUP
            hoverImage   =   "hover.bmp"
            downImage   =   "down.bmp"
            mappingImage   =   "map.bmp">

        <BUTTONELEMENT
            mappingColor   =   "#00FF00"
            onClick   =   "JScript:  player.URL   =   'file:laure.wma';"
            upToolTip   =   "Play"  />

        <BUTTONELEMENT
            mappingColor   =   "#FF0000"
            onClick   =   "JScript:  player.controls.stop();""
            upToolTip   =   "Stop"  />

        <BUTTONELEMENT
            mappingColor   =   "#0000FF"
            onClick   =   "JScript:  view.returnToMediaCenter();""
            upToolTip   =   "Return  to  Full  Mode"  />

        </BUTTONGROUP>

    </VIEW>
</THEME>
```

Now you have all the pieces put together. Use PKWARE's PKZIP or another program that compresses files into the ZIP format, to zip up your skin definition file (.wms), bitmaps, and any JScript files you have created, into one file. Rename the zipped file with the extension .wmz.

Your skin is ready to go!

Note   The skin you distribute must have the .wmz file name extension. If you distribute a compressed skin file with the .zip extension, the Player will not recognize or open it.

CHAPTER 9

Adding More to Skins

In Chapter 8 you learned how to build a simple skin. This chapter shows advanced techniques that focus on specific tasks. You'll be shown code examples for each technique as well as views of the various art needed. The following tasks will be covered:

- Adding a progress bar
- Adding a slider
- Adding a custom slider
- Adding a video window
- Adding a visualization
- Adding a sliding drawer
- Adding a dialog box for opening files
- Adding a playlist
- Adding text

Adding a progress bar

The **PROGRESSBAR** element displays incremental changes based on real-time events happening inside your skin or Windows Media Player. A progress bar is a horizontal or vertical bar that has a moving marker image to indicate the current value of whatever is being measured. The marker is called a *thumb*. A progress bar does not respond directly to user events such as mouse clicks. The most common use of a progress bar is to show the current position of the music or video that is playing. As the current position of the content changes, the position of the of the progress bar will match it.

Figure 9.1 shows a simple skin with a horizontal progress bar near the bottom of the skin. The thumb image is two-thirds of the way to the right of the bar. The skin also has two buttons which are used to start and stop the Player.

Figure 9.1 – *Progress bar example.*

Progress bar art files

The primary art file for the progress bar looks like Figure 9.2. For this example, the progress bar is not created in the art; it will be painted on the skin by Windows Media Player when the skin is displayed. However, you must leave room for the progress bar on your skin.

Figure 9.2 – *Primary art file for the progress bar.*

All progress bars must have a thumb image. The image is displayed on top of the progress bar. Figure 9.3 shows the thumb image.

Figure 9.3 – *Thumb image for the progress bar.*

In this example, the progress bar is painted on the skin by the Player, and the color is assigned by the **backgroundColor** attribute.

If you want to create a progress bar image, you can create a bitmap and assign it to the **backgroundImage** attribute of **PROGRESSBAR**. For example, if you created a bitmap for the background of the progress bar that looked like Figure 9.4, the resulting slider would look like Figure 9.5.

Figure 9.4 – *Background bitmap for a progress bar.*

Figure 9.5 – *Progress bar with the background image.*

Progress bar code

The following code segment can be used to create a progress bar:

```
<PROGRESSBAR
            enabled  =  "false"
            left  =  "40"
            top  =  "155"
            width  =  "220"
            height  =  "10"
            backgroundColor  =  "red"
            thumbImage  =  "thumb.bmp"
            min  =  "0"
            max  =  "wmpprop:player.currentMedia.duration"
            value  =  "wmpprop:player.controls.currentPosition"/>
```

The attributes were given their values for the following reasons:

enabled
>   You should set this to false. If set to true, and the user tries to drag the thumb, it will attempt to move and snap back.

left, top, width, height
>   These define the area of the progress bar rectangle. The height (in pixels) should be the same height as the thumb image. The width should be a multiple of the width of the thumb image.

backgroundColor
>   This is the color that the progress bar will be. If you want to use an image instead, use the **backgroundImage** property.

thumbImage
>   This is the name of the image file for the thumb image.

min

> This is the minimum value of the progress bar. When the value being measured is at the minimum, the thumb will be at the left end of the bar. In this case, it is zero.

max

> This is the maximum value of the progress bar. When the value being measured is at the maximum, the thumb will be at the right end of the bar. The maximum value is defined in code by listening with **wmpprop** to the value of the **duration** property as defined through the **currentMedia** property of the **Player** object.

value

> The **value** attribute is what must change to move the thumb image. The **value** is constantly updated by listening with **wmpprop** to the value of the **currentPosition** property of the **Controls** object.

You can find out more about the **PROGRESSBAR** element and its attributes in the Windows Media Player 7 SDK.

Adding a slider

Sliders are very similar to progress bars and share all the same attributes. The main difference between them is that sliders can be modified by interaction with the user. Sliders are often used for volume controls.

Sliders must be enabled; you can do this by setting the **enabled** attribute to true, or you can just leave it out, because the default value is true. You must also set up the slider so that it will respond to mouse clicks.

You can create a slider that allows the user to change the position of the current media stream. Moving the position of the media while it is playing is called *seeking*, and often sliders that do seeking are called seek bars or track bars. To turn the progress bar into a slider that seeks, all you have to do is take the progress bar example and make a few changes to the code. The artwork can be the same, because sliders also have a background and thumb image.

Remove the following line:

```
enabled = "false"
```

Add the following lines:

```
onmousedown="player.controls.currentPosition=value"
value_onchange="value    =    player.controls.currentPosition"
```

The attributes were given their values for the following reasons:

onmousedown
> This is an event handler that is called when a mouse-down event occurs. The line inside the quotes is executed and assigns the **value** of the slider position to the **currentPosition** property of the **Controls** object. If the user clicks the slider, the relative position is used to change the position of the content that is playing.

value_onchange
> This is an event handler that is called whenever the **value** attribute of the slider changes. The line inside the quotes is executed and assigns the **currentPosition** property of the **Controls** object to the **value** attribute. This ensures that whenever the **value** changes, it is instantly updated to reflect the new position of the current music or video. You do not need this line, but it makes for smoother seeking.

You can find out more about the **PROGRESSBAR** element and its attributes in the Windows Media Player 7 SDK.

Adding a custom slider

Custom sliders are very similar to sliders except that they do not need to be linear. For example, a custom slider can be used to create a volume control that slides along a curve. Or you can use a custom slider to create a knob that turns when you click it. Figure 9.6 shows a custom slider that is a single knob.

Figure 9.6 – *Custom slider that creates a knob.*

Custom slider art files

The primary art file is shown in Figure 9.7. Tiny + and – symbols were added to the skin to indicate that if the knob is turned to the left, the sound will be quieter, and to the right, louder.

Figure 9.7 – *Primary art file of the custom slider*

A custom slider has two special types of art. The first is the mapping image that tells Windows Media Player when a region of your skin is clicked. The mapping image is a bitmap with regions defined by grayscale values. If you want to define 13 different places to click, you must define 13 different regions with distinct gray color values.

In this custom slider example, the mapping image looks like Figure 9.8.

Figure 9.8 – *Custom slider mapping image.*

The gray regions range from total black on the left (#000000) to total white on the right (#FFFFFF). The 13 gray color values for the regions in this example are:

```
#000000
#151515
#2B2B2B
#404040
#555555
#6A6A6A
#808080
#959595
#AAAAAA
#BFBFBF
#D5D5D5
#EAEAEA
#FFFFFF
```

To create gray values, you must make the red, green, and blue two-digit hexadecimal values equal when you are combining them to make the six-digit hexadecimal color value. The values do not need to be evenly spread out, but they must be distinct and in increasing order.

After you have defined the mapping image, you are ready to create the custom slider art for the knob. Custom slider art consists of a bitmap that contains copies of all the different images you want to display. In the case of the knob, you will have thirteen images in the file. The custom knob art file looks like Figure 9.9.

Figure 9.9 – *Custom slider art file.*

When the user clicks the skin in the area defined by the darkest gray color, the image at the left of the custom slider art file will be displayed. When the user clicks the region defined by the lightest gray color, the image at the right end of the custom slider art file will be displayed. For regions in between, the corresponding portions of the custom slider art file will be displayed.

The custom slider art file must contain multiple images that will fit in the sizes defined by the code. You can create many interesting custom slider effects by using multiple images and different regions.

Custom slider code

The following code segment can be used to create a custom slider:

```
<CUSTOMSLIDER
          left="128"
          top="100"
          min="0"
          max="100"
          image="dial.bmp"
          positionImage="dialmap.bmp"
          transparencyColor="#00FFFF"
          value="wmpprop:player.settings.volume"
          value_onchange="player.settings.volume=value"
          />
```

The attributes were given their values for the following reasons:

left, top
> These two attributes define where the button will appear on the skin, based on the horizontal and vertical distances (in pixels) from the top left corner of the skin to the top left corner of the button.

min, max
> These are the minimum and maximum values of the custom slider. Because this is for a volume control, the minimum is zero and the maximum is 100.

image
> This is the file name of the bitmap that contains the multiple images for the custom slider. The images must be laid out in multiples of the height and width of the **positionImage** bitmap. For example, if the **positionImage** bitmap is 10 pixels by 10 pixels, and there were 15 images to be laid out horizontally, the **image** bitmap would be 150 pixels wide and 10 pixels high, with each image being 10 by 10. The images can be arranged either horizontally or vertically.

positionImage
> This is the file name of the bitmap that contains the grayscale mapping image for the custom slider.

transparencyColor
> This defines the color that will not be displayed in the **image** bitmap. This value is #00FFFF, which is the background color of the **image** bitmap.

value
> This changes the custom slider **value** by listening with **wmpprop** to changes in the **volume** property of the **Settings** object.

value_onchange
> This is an event handler that is called whenever the **value** attribute of the custom slider changes. The line inside the quotes is executed and assigns the current slider value to the **volume** property of the **Settings** object. This updates the Player and adjusts the volume based on the user changing the **value** of the custom slider.

Adding a video window

The **VIDEO** element displays the image from a video clip if one is playing. All you need to do is specify the location of the video window on your skin.

Figure 9.10 shows a simple skin with **Play** and **Stop** buttons, and a video window.

Figure 9.10 – *Simple skin with a video window.*

Video art files

The primary art file for the video example looks like Figure 9.11. The video window does not appear until the video starts playing. You might want to create a dark background where the video window will play to let the user know that video will be playing there.

Figure 9.11 – *Video art file.*

Video window code

The following code segment can be used to create a video window:

```
<VIDEO
        top  =  "10"
        left  =  "80"
        width  =  "180"
        height  =  "180"/>
```

The attributes were given their values for the following reasons:

top, left, width, height
    These set the position and size of the video window on the skin.

You can find out more about the **VIDEO** element and its attributes in the Windows Media Player 7 SDK.

Adding a visualization

The **EFFECTS** element displays a visualization in a window on the skin. Figure 9.12 shows a visualization in a window.

Figure 9.12 – *Simple visualization window.*

Visualizations are normally displayed in a rectangular window. If you would like to mask off part of a visualization to create a non-rectangular view, you can use a masking image. See Figure 9.13 for a masked visualization window.

Figure 9.13 – *Masked visualization window.*

Visualization art files

The primary art file for a visualization is a simple skin with buttons to change the presets. If the visualization has a default image, it will appear when the skin is applied. Figure 9.14 shows the primary art file for a visualization.

Figure 9.14 – *Primary art file for a visualization.*

You can add a clipping image like Figure 9.15 if you want a non-rectangular shape for your visualization.

Figure 9.15 – *Clipping image for the visualization.*

In this example, the color inside the circle (black) will be the part of the visualization that shows through, and the color outside of the circle (white) will clip off the visualization.

Visualization code

The following code segment can be used to create a visualization window. The name of the element that displays visualizations is called the **EFFECTS** element.

```
<EFFECTS
          id = "myeffects"
          top = "25"
          left = "88"
          width = "180"
          height = "150"/>
```

The attributes were given their values for the following reasons:

top, left, width, height
    These set the position and size of the visualization window on the skin.

If you want to add a clipping image, add the following line:

```
clippingImage = "clip.bmp"
```

The value of the **clippingImage** attribute should be the file name of your clipping image.

You can find out more about the **EFFECTS** element and its attributes in the Windows Media Player 7 SDK.

Adding a sliding drawer

Sliding drawers are a way to hide parts of the user interface until they are needed. If you offer every option to the user all the time, a skin can be too cluttered. The default skin of the Player shows a good example of how drawers work. When you first see the default skin, it looks like Figure 9.16.

Figure 9.16 – *The default skin.*

However, if you click the tabs on the right or bottom edges of the default skin, drawers pop out that display the current playlist or the current settings. Figure 9.17 shows the default skin with its drawers open.

You can use drawers to contain user interface elements such as equalizer settings, playlists, videos, visualizations, and so on.

Figure 9.17 – *Default skin with open drawers.*

The easiest way to achieve a drawer effect is to create two subviews and have the drawer be one view and the main skin elements be the other. A simple skin that uses a drawer is shown in Figure 9.18.

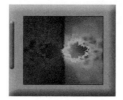

Figure 9.18 – *Simple drawer skin.*

When the handle is clicked on the left, the drawer opens, showing the buttons for **Next Preset** and **Previous Preset**. See the open drawer in Figure 9.19.

Figure 9.19 – *Open drawer.*

Drawer art files

The primary art file for this example looks like Figure 9.20. Note that the edge on the left side is not beveled.

Figure 9.20 – *Primary art file.*

The art file for the drawer looks like Figure 9.21.

Figure 9.21 – *Drawer art file.*

When the two files are displayed, the primary art will be on top of the drawer art, cutting off most of it except the drawer handle. Then, when the handle is clicked, the drawer will slide out, exposing the two buttons.

Drawer code

The coding for this skin with a drawer is accomplished by using two subviews, one for each piece of art.

The first subview is used to display the visualization and the background image.

```
<SUBVIEW
        left = "80"
        clippingColor  =  "#FFFFFF"
        backgroundImage  =  "background.bmp"
        zIndex = "5">

        <EFFECTS
            id = "myeffects"
            top = "25"
            left = "12"
            width = "180"
            height = "150"/>


</SUBVIEW>
```

The attributes of the first **SUBVIEW** element are given their values for the following reasons:

left
> This sets this view 80 pixels left of the left edge of the skin, giving room for the button that opens the drawer to show through.

id

This is defined as "myeffects" because it will be referred to later by the JScript code for the two buttons that change to the next or previous visualizations.

clippingColor

The clipping color is defined to be white.

backgroundImage

This is the file name of the bitmap that contains the background image.

zIndex

The **zIndex** determines which element is displayed in front of another. Because the value of this subview's **zIndex** is 5, it will be displayed in front of the other view, which has a **zIndex** that is not defined and therefore zero.

The **EFFECTS** element defines the visualization window.

The second subview displays three buttons, the right two of which are initially hidden.

```
<SUBVIEW
          id = "drawer"
          left = "60"
          backgroundImage="drawer.bmp"
          transparencyColor="#000000">

          <BUTTONGROUP
             mappingImage  =  "map.bmp"
             hoverImage    =  "hover.bmp">

             <BUTTONELEMENT
                mappingColor   =  "#00FF00"
                onClick   =   "JScript:myeffects.next();"/>

             <BUTTONELEMENT
                mappingColor   =  "#FF0000"
                onClick   =   "JScript:myeffects.previous();"/>

             <BUTTONELEMENT
                mappingColor   =  "#0000FF"
                onClick   =   "JScript:moveDrawer();"/>

          </BUTTONGROUP>

</SUBVIEW>
```

The attributes of the second **SUBVIEW** element are given their values for the following reasons:

id

> This view needs an **id** attribute defined because it will be referred to later by some JScript code. Give it a descriptive, easy-to-remember name such as "drawer".

left

> The initial value of the **left** attribute for the drawer is 60 pixels left of the left edge of the skin. The normal left edge of the drawer view would be at the left edge of the background image of the view, but by defining the left edge of this drawer view at 60, it makes the absolute edge of the skin 60 pixels farther to the left than it would have been without the drawer.

backgroundImage

> The bitmap that is used for this view is the drawer image itself.

transparencyColor

> The transparency color is is defined as black.

The three buttons use the standard **BUTTONGROUP** and **BUTTONELEMENT** elements. The first two buttons call the **next** and **previous** methods on the visualization in the other view, but the third button calls a JScript function called **moveDrawer** which is defined in a separate JScript file.

The **moveDrawer** function is defined in a JScript file that was loaded when the skin was applied. You can load JScript files by giving them the same file name as the skin, but with the file name extension of .js.

The JScript file contains the following code.

```
var isOpen = false;

function moveDrawer() {
        if (isOpen) {
            drawer.moveTo(60,0,500);
            drawerButton.upToolTip = "Show Controls";
            isOpen = false;
        } else {
            drawer.moveTo(0,0,500);
            drawerButton.upToolTip = "Hide Controls";
            isOpen = true;
        }
}
```

First the **isOpen** variable is defined and given the value false. Then when the **moveDrawer** function is called, a test is made to see if the drawer is open. It won't be open the first time, so the drawer view will be moved using the **moveTo** method. The ToolTip is defined to read "Hide Controls", **isOpen** is defined as true, and the function exits.

The next time **moveDrawer** is called, the value of **isOpen** will be true, so the drawer will be closed with a call to **moveTo**, the ToolTip will read "Show Controls", and the value of **isOpen** will be defined as false. The function will toggle back and forth each time it is called.

You can also display drawers by simply hiding and showing parts of a skin. For example, if you define the height of a skin as 175 pixels in the **VIEW** element, you can use code to redefine the height as taller by using code such as the following:

```
if (view.height==200) {
        view.height='400';
} else {
        view.height='200';
}
```

Figure 9.22 shows a simple video skin with a hidden drawer.

Figure 9.22 – *Simple video skin with hidden drawer.*

When you click the video window, a drawer opens showing the playlist. Figure 9.23 shows the skin with the drawer open.

This was created by adding a simple **PLAYLIST** element that is displayed on the lower half of the background image. The playlist is on the skin but you don't see it until the JScript code is called that changes the skin height to 400, exposing the hidden part of the skin. The code was activated by using an **onClick** event for the **VIDEO** element.

Figure 9.23 – *Playlist drawer for a simple video.*

For this example, the background image looks like Figure 9.24. But only the top portion is seen when the skin is first applied.

Figure 9.24 – *Background image of hidden drawer skin.*

There are many good books on JScript that you can read to learn more about techniques like the code above. You can find out more about the **SUBVIEW** element and its attributes in the Windows Media Player 7 SDK.

Adding a dialog box for opening files

If you want to add an **Open** dialog box to your skin for opening files, all you have to do is call the following line from an event such as **onClick** in a button:

```
onClick="JScript:player.URL=theme.openDialog('FILE_OPEN','FILES_ALL');
```

A typical **Open** dialog box looks like Figure 9.25.

Figure 9.25 – *Open dialog box.*

Adding a playlist

You can add playlists to your skin easily by using the **PLAYLIST** element. Figure 9.26 shows a simple skin without a playlist.

Figure 9.26 – *Skin without a playlist.*

When you click the right button, a separate window will appear with a playlist. Figure 9.27 shows the new playlist window. You do not need any art files to display a playlist; the **PLAYLIST** element will display the playlist as a window.

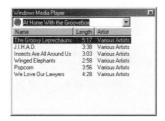

Figure 9.27 – *Playlist window.*

Playlist code

There are two views in the skin definition file. The first view will display the buttons and the background. The second view will be displayed in a separate window and will contain the playlist.

In order to display the second view, you must trigger the following line with an event like **onClick**.

```
onClick  =  "JScript:  theme.openView('playview');"
```

The second view has an **id** attribute of "playview". When it is opened, it will display a default playlist using the code below.

```
<VIEW
        id = "playview">
        <PLAYLIST/>
</VIEW>
```

The view has only one element in it, which is a default **PLAYLIST** element.

You can find out more about the **PLAYLIST** and **VIEW** elements and their attributes in the Windows Media Player 7 SDK.

Adding text

You can add text to any skin with the **TEXT** element. All you need to do is specify the location and values of the **TEXT** element. In fact, you can use **TEXT** elements to do anything that buttons can do, because a **TEXT** element can handle events. Figure 9.28 shows a skin that contains no art at all, but uses **TEXT** elements to do everything.

Figure 9.28 – *A skin that uses all text and no original art.*

Text code

This text-based skin uses several text windows. The windows labeled "Play", "Stop", and "Close" will start, stop, and close the Player when they are clicked.

For example, the code for the Play text window looks like this:

```
<TEXT
            width = "150"
            fontSize = "30"
            hoverFontStyle = "Bold"
            hoverForegroundColor = "red"
            justification = "Center"
            value = "Play"
            cursor = "hand"
            onClick        =JScript:player.URL='file:.\\..\\media\\laure.wma';"
/>
```

The attributes of this **TEXT** element are given their values for the following reasons:

width

This defines the width of the text window.

fontSize

This defines the size of the font.

hoverFontStyle

When the user hovers a cursor over the text window, the font will change to bold, indicating that a click will have an effect.

hoverForegroundColor

When the user hovers a cursor over the text window, the color of the font will turn red, indicating that a click will have an effect.

justification

This centers the text in the window.

value

The value is the text to be displayed in the window.

cursor

By displaying a hand cursor when the user hovers over the text windows, the skin indicates that something can be done by clicking the window.

onClick

This event handler will start the Player playing a particular song called "laure.wma".

The other text windows are set up in a similar manner.

The "+" window changes the volume using code like this:

```
onClick  =  "player.settings.volume  =  player.settings.volume  +  5"
```

The "-" window is similar but subtracts 5 from the current volume.

The "Volume" window displays the current volume but doesn't change it.

There is a scrolling window at the bottom of the screen that uses the following lines to scroll the Player status like a marquee:

```
scrolling  =  "true"
scrollingAmount  =  "1"
scrollingDelay  =  "50"
value  =  "wmpprop:player.status"
```

This skin has a menu bar at the top and an outline. Both were created by the following code:

```
<VIEW
            height  =  "175"
    >
```

All the other skins shown in this chapter require that the **titleBar** attribute of the **VIEW** element be set to false. By not including it in this view, the default value of true is assumed, and the skin will have a title bar. The height was set at 175 because the default height of 200 was not the desired spacing. The default width is 300 pixels.

Going further

As you experiment with skins, you will be able to gradually expand on the methods and effects demonstrated in this chapter. There are three basic ways you can increase your knowledge and skill with skin programming.

1. Study skins created by other people. You can unzip any skin and study the code in the skin definition file as well as the code in any JScript files present.

2. Browse through the Skin Programming Reference portion of the Windows Media Player 7 SDK. You will find elements and attributes that you may not have been aware of.

3. Look for future articles on skin creation at the MSDN Web site, at other sites, and in programming and Web design magazines.

CHAPTER 10

Testing and Distributing Skins

Chapters 6, 7, 8, and 9 showed you how to create skins. This chapter will focus on how to test and distribute your skins.

Testing skins

There are two times you will want to test skins:

- While you are creating them, particularly when you're not sure what's going on inside your skin.

- When you are done.

Analyzing what is going on inside your skin

Chapter 7 discussed writing the code as part of the overall four-step skin design process. Writing code for a skin involves two general steps, one for each language:

1. Write the XML tags for all the user interface elements of your skin.

2. Add the JScript code to connect the user interface to the Player.

Write and test XML functionality first

You might want to write and test your XML first. By doing this, you'll avoid confusion later in situations where you're not sure whether the error is in your XML code or your JScript code. The following steps will help you write and test your XML code.

Using a shell

One way to write your skin code is to create your skin definition file and put all your XML tags in it. You might want to start with the following shell:

```
<THEME>
   <VIEW
       clippingColor  =  "#000000"
       backgroundImage  =  "background.bmp"
       titleBar  =  "false">
   </VIEW>
</THEME>
```

Of course, you'll want to be sure that you change the clipping color if you don't want it to be black.

Adding the XML tags

Add all the XML tags but don't add any event handlers (**onClick**, **value_onChange**, and so on). A simple two-button skin without any event handlers might look like this:

```
<THEME>
   <VIEW
       clippingColor  =  "#CCCC00"
       backgroundImage  =  "background.bmp"
       titleBar  =  "false">

           <BUTTONGROUP
               mappingImage  =  "map.bmp"
               hoverImage  =  "hover.bmp">

               <BUTTONELEMENT
                   mappingColor  =  "#00FF00"/>

               <BUTTONELEMENT
                   mappingColor  =  "#FF0000"/>

           </BUTTONGROUP>

   </VIEW>
</THEME>
```

Testing your XML

You are then ready to do a functional test. Assuming you have the art files in the proper location, double-click the name of your skin definition file and see what happens. If all goes well, you will see your skin.

This does not guarantee that all your XML code is correct. If you break one of the XML rules, you will get an error message similar to Figure 10.1.

Figure 10.1 – *Missing end-tag error message.*

Figure 10.1 shows the error message you will get if you don't have a closing **BUTTONGROUP** tag. All your tags must be in opening and closing pairs like this:

```
<BUTTONGROUP>

</BUTTONGROUP>
```

Or you must close off an element if there are no other elements nested within the element. For example, you'll always have **BUTTONELEMENT** elements nested inside a **BUTTONGROUP** element, but you probably won't have elements nested inside each **BUTTONELEMENT**. Because of this, each **BUTTONELEMENT** can be closed without a closing tag by using the slash after your attributes but before the closing angle bracket.

```
<BUTTONELEMENT
        mappingColor="#00FF00"/>
```

If you misspell a closing element name, you'll get an error similar to Figure 10.2.

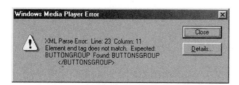

Figure 10.2 – *Misspelled element name.*

However, if you misspell an element name and do not have a separate closing tag, the XML parser won't catch your mistake. For example, if you type BUTTONSELEMENT, you won't get an error if you close off the tag with a slash at the end of the element name.

For this reason, it is recommended that you always have an opening tag and a closing tag, so that the error messages can help you find any typing errors.

If you leave out the value of an attribute, you'll get an error similar to Figure 10.3.

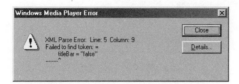

Figure 10.3 – *Missing attribute value.*

The code that generated this error looks like this:

```
clippingColor  =  "#CCCC00"
backgroundImage
titleBar = "false"
```

There is no value after the **backgroundImage** attribute. The error message points to the line after the missing value of **backgroundImage**. Sometimes the error handling system cannot determine the exact line that contains the error. If you don't understand where the error occurred, look at the line before or after the one indicated in the error message.

There are many other possible XML errors that can be generated. But by testing your skin before you add event handlers, you'll eliminate simple XML errors right away.

Write and test JScript functionality next

After you have tested your XML, add your event handlers for each user interface element and test them.

Writing handlers

Handlers respond to events. An event can come from a user action (such as pressing a key or clicking the mouse) or something happening inside Windows Media Player (such as the track coming to an end).

Event handlers have two parts: the event name and the code that will be run. The event name is the type of event (**click**, **keydown**, and so on) with the word "on" in front of it. The event name is treated like an attribute and assigned a value. The value is a string that will be executed when the event occurs. For example, the handler that would start the Player if you clicked on the element would look like this:

```
onClick = "JScript: player.controls.play();"
```

You can also have an event that is triggered when any attribute changes value. Take the attribute name and add "_onchange" to it. For example, if the value of a slider with the **id** attribute "myslider" changed, you could create an event to change the volume of the Player with the following code.

```
value_onChange = "JScript: player.settings.volume = myslider.value;"
```

You can respond to events in the Player by using the **wmpprop** listener keyword. For example, to set the value of a progress bar to the value of the current volume, you would use a handler like the following:

```
value = "wmpprop: player.settings.volume"
```

Note that **wmpprop** is used for listening to the value of properties. If you want to listen to methods in the Player to see whether a method is enabled, use **wmpenabled** and **wmpdisabled**.

The best way to study handlers is to look at all the events that are listed in the Skin Programming Reference section of the Windows Media Player 7 SDK. You will also want to study other skins to see which events are handled and how. As well as using the SDK, you'll want to find a good reference on JScript so that you can understand JScript grammar and syntax.

Testing handlers

You might want to add error handlers for one button at a time and see whether what you think should happen actually does. For example, create the event you want to happen when the user clicks the **Play** button. A simple handler to process a click event and start the Player might look like the following:

```
onClick = "JScript:player.URL = '.\\..\\media\\laure.wma';"
```

As you create each handler, start the Player and click the appropriate button or control. Unfortunately, some errors can't be found easily. If you type

```
onClick = "JScript:plaxer.WRL = '.\\..\\media\\laure.wma';"
```

you won't get an error message. The Player won't play because you mis-spelled "player" and "URL". The parser doesn't know what you mean, but you aren't breaking any rules. It assumes that you are creating a new JScript variable instead of assigning a value to a **Player** property.

Player errors

If you cause an error in the core functionality of the Player, you will get an error message. For example, if you try to tell the Player to find a file that doesn't exist, you'll get an error message similar to Figure 10.4.

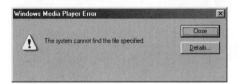

Figure 10.4 – *Missing-file error.*

You can get more details about specific errors by clicking the **Details** button. Figure 10.5 shows the information you will receive if you click the **Details** button of the missing-file error message.

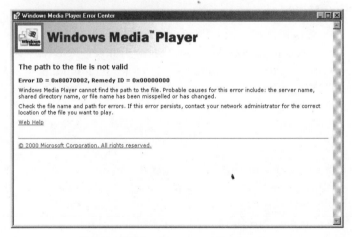

Figure 10.5 – *Missing-file details.*

JScript errors

If you make an error in JScript syntax, you will get an error similar to Figure 10.6.

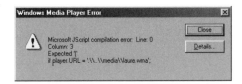

Figure 10.6 – *JScript error.*

The line that caused the error had the JScript keyword **if** inserted before the word "player". This caused a simple error because it doesn't follow the syntax rules of JScript.

If you get JScript errors, you can study the online documentation for JScript as well as books on JScript and similar scripting languages, to understand how to fix a particular error.

Finding logic errors

If you did not make any Player or JScript or XML errors, the error is most likely in the logic of the code you have written. One of the best ways to test the logic of your code is to see what is happening as your code is processed.

Using TEXT output

The best way to catch errors that don't generate error messages is to "see" your code in action by displaying messages on your skin with the **TEXT** element.

For example, suppose you are working on a skin that has two buttons and a progress bar. The code might look like this:

```
<THEME>
    <VIEW
        clippingColor    =    "#FFFFFF"
        backgroundImage  =    "background.bmp"
        titleBar = "False"
    >
        <BUTTONGROUP
            mappingImage=    "map.bmp"
            hoverImage=    "hover.bmp"
            >
```

```
            <BUTTONELEMENT
                onClick  =  "JScript:plaxer.URL  =  'file:laure.wma';"
                mappingColor  =  "#00FF00"
                />

            <BUTTONELEMENT
                onClick  =  "JScript:  view.close();""
                mappingColor  =  "#FF0000"
                />

        </BUTTONGROUP>

        <PROGRESSBAR
            enabled  =  "false"
            cursor  =  "system"
            left  =  "40"
            top  =  "155"
            width  =  "220"
            height  =  "10"
            tooltip  =  "Current  position"
            backgroundColor  =  "red"
            thumbImage  =  "thumb.bmp"
            min  =  "0"
            max    =    "wmpprop:player.currentMedia.duration"
            value    =    "wmpprop:player.controls.currentPosition"
            />


        </VIEW>
    </THEME>
```

The skin will look like Figure 10.7.

Figure 10.7 – *Skin with a progress bar.*

If you click the **Play** button, nothing happens. The Player doesn't play, and it doesn't display an error message either. But you can test what is going on inside your skin by adding a **TEXT** element such as the following:

```
<TEXT
    id = "bugbox"
    left = "75"
    top = "25"
    width = "100"
    justification = "right"
    fontStyle = "bold"
    />
```

You now have an invisible window on your skin. All you have to do is assign a value to the **TEXT** element to display information about what is going on with your code. One of the easy ways to do this is to create a separate JScript file and call a function that displays a message. To create a JScript file, create a text file with the same name as the skin file but with the extension .js. For example, if your skin definition file is called myskin.wms, your JScript file will be called myskin.js and will be loaded when your skin is loaded.

Now create a function in your JScript file called **showme**.

```
function showme() {
    bugbox.value = "CLICK";
}
```

Then, insert the function **showme** into the handler you are testing. Where it used to read:

```
onClick = "JScript:plaxer.URL = 'file:laure.wma';"
```

make it read

```
onClick = "JScript:showme();plaxer.URL = 'file:laure.wma';"
```

The function name, **showme**, must be followed by parentheses and be separated from any other statements by a semicolon.

Now, when you click the button, your skin will look like Figure 10.8.

Figure 10.8 – *Skin with text on it.*

This tells you that the first part of the handler is working properly, because the click event was triggered. So the problem is inside the handler but after the place where you inserted **showme**.

Next, put **showme** after the other handler statements so the line looks like this:

```
onClick  =  "JScript:plaxer.URL  =  'file:laure.wma';showme();"
```

Now when you click the **Play** button, nothing happens. This indicates that the statement before **showme** was not executed properly. If you look at the line more carefully, you'll see that the word "player" was misspelled "plaxer". If you fix it, the word "CLICK" will appear on the skin, indicating that the line was executed properly.

You can also use **TEXT** elements to print out changing values. For example, you could display the value of the progress bar by adding the following code to the **PROGRESSBAR** element:

```
id  =  "mybar"
value_onChange  =  "bugbox.value  =  mybar.value"
```

You must assign an **id** to the progress bar first so you can reference it in the **value_onChange** handler.

There are many other ways you can use a **TEXT** element to find out what is going on in your skin. For example, you can use it to monitor values in the Player (using **wmpprop**), events that are caused by the user, or changes in the attributes of user interface elements.

Using the Error object

You can also detect errors by using the **Error** object. For example, if you think an error has occurred, and you are still able to process errors, you can get a description of the error by using the following code:

```
player.error.item(index).errorDescription
```

where *index* is the particular error you are curious about in the queue of errors. For example, if there are three errors that have occurred in your skin, you could get the first error by setting the index to zero.

See the Windows Media Player SDK for more information about using the **Error** object.

Using logging

If you are creating complex skins, consider using an advanced feature of the Player called logging. Logging lets you write messages to a file on your hard disk that you can read with a text editor. The purpose of logging is that it lets you see messages similar to what you would see with the **TEXT** element, but doesn't interfere with the look of your skin.

To use logging, you must get two files from the Windows Media Player Player SDK. They are called debugon.reg and debugoff.reg. In Windows Explorer, double-click debugon.reg to start logging and double-click debugoff.reg to turn it off. You will get a dialog box each time you enable or disable logging, asking whether you want to make changes to the registry. Click Yes. You will get a second message informing you that changes have been made.

If logging is enabled, a file will be placed on the hard disk in the same folder as the skin. The file will be named filename_0_log.txt, where filename is the name of the skin file. The code in your skin can write text to this file using the **Theme.logString** attribute. This can be useful if you want to determine what is going on inside your code while it is running.

The text file is composed of Unicode characters. For this and other reasons, it is recommended that you edit and develop professional skins with Microsoft Visual InterDev. If you use a simple ASCII text editor like Microsoft Windows Notepad, your text will look like Figure 10.9, because the editor is not intended for use with Unicode.

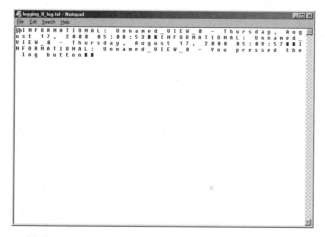

Figure 10.9 – *Unicode as displayed by an ASCII text editor.*

Code such as the following can be used to send text to the logger:

```
onClick = "JScript: theme.logString('You pressed the log button');"
```

You must use single quotation marks whenever you are inside an event handler.

Using Microsoft Visual InterDev

Microsoft Visual InterDev is a programming environment for Internet development. Even though skins are not Web pages, you can use Visual InterDev for skins in two ways: as an authoring environment and as a debugger.

Authoring with Visual InterDev

Visual InterDev makes writing code for skins easier. Visual InterDev can color code elements, attributes, values, and comments in a skin file. Just add your WMS file to your files list, making sure that your file is closed and added to the project. Then right-click the file name in Project Explorer, click **Open With**, and select **HTML Editor**.

You can also use the same option for JScript files by using the following as the first line of every .js file:

```
//<script>
```

Open your JScript files the same way, using the **HTML Editor** option of Visual InterDev. Not only will you get color coding for your JScript code, but you will get drop-down tips about JScript as you are coding.

Debugging with Visual InterDev

You can also use Visual InterDev as a professional debugging environment. After you have installed Visual InterDev, turn on script debugging by using the debugon.reg registry file. Then, when you run your skin and it has a JScript error, Visual InterDev will start up and take you to the line where your error occurred. You can set breakpoints, test your code, and understand more about what is happening inside the JScript portion of your skin code. Visual InterDev cannot debug the XML portion of your skin code, though it can provide color coding and other advanced text-editing features.

Being sure your skin is complete

When you have created all the user interface elements and added all the event handlers, your skin should be complete. Now comes the fun part. You must sit down and test every possible thing that can be done to your skin. Click every button in every order you can think of. Try all the combinations, because your user will.

Also test that all your secondary images appear as they should (hover and down images). Be sure any drawers you have added extend and retract as you intend them to. Check any other additions you've made to the basic skin.

Then, ask your friends to test your skins. They may think of things you haven't. Ask people who test your skin to take notes of what they do, so that if an error occurs, they'll be able to tell you how to reproduce the error.

Distributing skins

After your skin is finished, and you've tested every possible aspect of it, you're ready to distribute it.

Zipping it up

You must compress your skin using the ZIP format. Include the following items:

- Your skin definition file (with the .wms extension)
- All artwork for your skin
- Any JScript files that go with your skin

Then rename your compressed file so that the extension is .wmz. All skins must be distributed with the .wmz file extension.

> **Note**   The skin you distribute must have the .wmz file name extension. If you distribute a compressed skin file with the .zip extension, the Player will not recognize or open it.

For more information about ZIP compression, visit the PKWARE Web site at

http://www.pkware.com/

File preparation checklist

When preparing your final skin file, be sure you follow these procedures:

- The contents of your skin must include the skin definition file (with the .wms file extension), all artwork files, and any JScript files. Don't leave out the skin definition file.

- You must zip up the contents of your skin into a single file. Do not distribute skins in an uncompressed state or as a collection of files. Distribute one file per skin.

- The skin you distribute must have the .wmz file extension. If you distribute a compressed skin file with the .wms file extension, the Player will not open it.

- The .wms file extension is to be used for development purposes only and should not be used to distribute skins. Future versions of Windows Media Player may not support the .wms file extension. For this release, however, the skin definition file must have the .wms extension, but must be inside the compressed .wmz file.

Testing it again

After you've zipped up your skin, it should be tested again. Be sure you click all the buttons and that all the primary and secondary art images appear as you intended them to. You might ask your friends to test the final file again.

Also, put your single compressed skin (with the .wmz file name extension) on a different computer than the one you created it on. Be sure that computer has Windows Media Player 7 on it as well. Then double-click the skin to be sure it loads properly. To be certain you are not accidentally using any uncompressed files, don't copy the .wms file, the art files, or any JScript files to the new machine.

Sending it out

After you're sure your skin is completely tested, take a day off, and then go back and look at it one last time. When you're ready to send it out into the world, submit it to the Windows Media Skins Gallery. For more information on how to submit your skin for distribution, visit the Windows Media Web site at:

http://www.windowsmedia.com/

Part 3
Advanced Topics

CHAPTER 11

Using Windows Media Player
in a Web Page

Windows Media Player provides the technology to make your Web pages come alive with sound, video, and visualizations. By using Microsoft ActiveX technology, you can take the core Player functionality and use the programming power of Microsoft Internet Explorer to create complete multimedia Web applications.

Getting started

Windows Media Player makes the Web more than just text and graphics. You can add sound and video to your Web pages with only a few lines of code. Visitors to your site can listen to music while they browse, or you can let them pick specific audio and video selections from a playlist.

There are three ways to use the Player in a Web page:

In the background
> You can use this option if you just want to use the Player to play background music while people visit your site. You can create a playlist to change the tunes, repeat the playlist selections, or shuffle them. People won't know Windows Media Player is playing the music unless you tell them. If they don't have the Player installed on their computer, they will need to install it.

As a simple default interface
> You can provide your visitors with a simple user interface to the Player. They can use the normal transport controls of **Play**, **Stop**, **Fast Forward**, and so on, and watch videos or visualizations on the default window.

With a custom interface

If you want to go beyond the default Player interface for Web pages, you can create your own complete custom interface by using Internet Explorer technologies such as dynamic HTML (DHTML), ActiveX custom controls, VML, and more.

A simple Web page might look like Figure 11.1.

Figure 11.1 – *Simple Web page.*

You can add the Player to a Web page without displaying any visible controls to the user. This is a good option if you just want to play music on your Web page, especially if you want to create sequences of music with playlists. Figure 11.2 shows a simple Web page, with the Player playing in the background. You're not obligated to tell people where the music is coming from, but you might want to.

Figure 11.2 – *Simple Web page with music playing in the background.*

Windows Media Player offers a default user interface for Web pages. Figure 11.3 shows a page with the default interface. You'll recognize the style of buttons and sliders from the full mode of Windows Media Player, but everything is a bit simpler and more streamlined.

Figure 11.3 – *Web page with the default Player user interface.*

When a visitor clicks the **Play** button (on the lower left corner of the Player), the Player will start playing and will show a visualization. Figure 11.4 shows the Player in action in a Web page.

Figure 11.4 – *The Player in a Web page, playing music and showing a visual-ization.*

If you want to show your visitors a movie on your Web site, you can use the Player. Figure 11.5 shows a movie playing in a Web page.

Figure 11.5 – *The Player showing a movie in a Web page.*

You can also choose which controls to show at the bottom of the Player window. The view you saw in Figure 11.4 has all the controls. You can specify a "mini" set of controls that will make the image look like Figure 11.6.

Figure 11.6 – *The Player with minimum controls.*

The "mini" version of the Player in a Web page only has the **Play/Pause**, **Stop**, **Mute**, and **Volume** controls.

You can also create a version that has no controls but does have a window for displaying visualizations or videos. Figure 11.7 shows the embedded Player with no controls.

Figure 11.7 – *The Player with a visualization/video window but without controls.*

You can also change the size of the Player window, with or without controls, to fit your Web page design. Figure 11.8 shows a smaller window.

Figure 11.8 – *Web page with the Player in a smaller window.*

You're not limited to one song or video on a Web page. You can have several clips running at the same time. Figure 11.9 shows three different windows in the same Web page; each window is playing something different.

Figure 11.9 – *Three different audio and video windows running in the same page.*

If you don't like the default user interface that comes with the Player, you are free to create your own user interface that is only limited by your imagination and resources. You can use all the technology that comes with Internet Explorer to create new user interfaces such as Figure 11.10. For more informa-

tion about user interface technologies available in Internet Explorer, see the
MSDN Web Workshop at the MSDN Web site:

http://msdn.microsoft.com/

Figure 11.10 – *Custom user interface for the Player in a Web page.*

Setting up your Web page

Using the Player in a Web page involves three different technologies:
ActiveX, HTML, and JScript. You must also understand the core technology
of Windows Media Player, which is contained in an ActiveX control.

Using ActiveX

The core functionality of Windows Media Player has been distilled into a
software library called an ActiveX control. ActiveX controls are programs
that cannot run by themselves, but must be used by another program. A control is made up of one or more objects. Each object has one or more methods, properties, and events. By calling various methods, setting the values of
specific properties, and responding to events, you can write code that tells a
control what to do.

ActiveX is part of the Component Object Model (COM) technology, and
there are many books and articles on the subject. You can learn more about
COM and ActiveX from the MSDN Web Workshop at the Microsoft MSDN
Web site:

http://msdn.microsoft.com/

Windows Media Player provides several objects that divide the functionality of the Player. For example, the **Settings** object has properties to change the **Volume** and decide whether to **AutoStart** when loading, the **Controls** object has methods to **Play** and **Stop** the media, and the **Player** object can monitor events such as **MediaChange** and **Error** to determine when something important has happened. A chart of the object model used by the Player to expose all its functionality is in the Windows Media Player 7 SDK, which is included on the companion CD that comes with this book.

Using the OBJECT element of HTML

In order to use the Player control in a Web page, you must use the **OBJECT** element of HTML. The **OBJECT** element is used to notify Internet Explorer that you wish to use the Player control, and gives you a chance to initialize the control. You must assign values to specific attributes of the **OBJECT** element.

The following attributes must be defined for the **OBJECT** element:

id

> This attribute is a string of characters that defines a unique name for the Player object so that it can be called by code in your Web page. You can choose any name as long as no other object or element has the same name. If you have more than one **OBJECT** element in your page, each one must have a different **id** attribute.

classid

> This attribute consists of the word "CLSID", a colon, and a unique 32-digit hexadecimal number that identifies COM objects to the operating system. The Windows Media Player ActiveX control has the **classid** of "CLSID:6BF52A52-394A-11D3-B153-00C04F79FAA6". Do not try to type this number when you are creating the **OBJECT** element; cut and paste it from the Windows Media Player 7 SDK. If you get the number wrong, Internet Explorer will not be able to use the Player control.

In addition, you may want to define the **height** and **width** attributes as zero if you do not want the default user interface that the Player provides in a Web page.

You can also define some initial values for the Player control by using **PARAM** elements, which are nested inside the **OBJECT** element. You can

have as many **PARAM** tags inside an **OBJECT** element as you want.
PARAM has two attributes, **name** and **value**. Both attributes must be set. You
can use **PARAM** elements to define whether you want the Player to start
when the control is loaded, the initial volume setting, the mode of the default
user interface, and so on. For more information on what you can define
through **PARAM** elements, see the Windows Media Player 7 SDK.

The following example shows a typical Player **OBJECT** element with attributes.

```
<OBJECT  id="Player"
    classid="CLSID:6BF52A52-394A-11d3-B153-00C04F79FAA6">
        <PARAM   name="URL"    value=".\\..\\media\\laure.wma">
        <PARAM   name="AutoStart"   value="False">
</OBJECT>
```

This **OBJECT** code sets up the Player to display a default user interface but
not start playing until the user clicks the **Play** button. When the user clicks
the **Play** button, the file named laure.wma will start playing.

Defining the user interface with HTML

If you don't want to use the default user interface that comes with the Player
control, you must create your own. Internet Explorer provides a variety of
ways to do this. You can choose from the following options and more.

Using forms

One of the easiest ways to define a user interface is with HTML **FORM** elements. For example, to create two buttons on your Web page, use the following code:

```
<FORM>
<INPUT   TYPE="BUTTON"   NAME="BtnPlay"   VALUE="Play"   OnClick="StartMeUp()">
<INPUT   TYPE="BUTTON"   NAME="BtnStop"   VALUE="Stop"   OnClick="ShutMeDown()">
</FORM>
```

This will create two buttons. If you hide the default user interface of the
Player control by setting the height and width to zero, the Web page will look
like Figure 11.11.

Figure 11.11 – *Simple Web page interface with two buttons.*

The attribute **OnClick** is called an *event* and will call a function with the defined name when the element is clicked. The first INPUT button will call a JScript function named **StartMeUp**, and the second button will call another function called **ShutMeDown**. These functions are called *event handlers* because they "handle" events by calling a code segment when an event is triggered. Details about JScript functions will be covered in the "Implementing event handlers" section later in this chapter.

Using SPAN elements for text buttons

Instead of using **FORM** buttons, you can take advantage of DHTML by using the **SPAN** element to mark off portions of a paragraph and assign image handlers to each portion.

For example, you could use **SPAN** elements to mark off the words "Play" and "Stop" in a paragraph. When the user clicks the specific word, an event is triggered that will start or stop the Player.

Use the following code to create this effect:

```
<SPAN    onclick=StartMeUp()><B>PLAY</B></SPAN>
<SPAN    onclick=ShutMeDown()><B>STOP</B></SPAN>
```

Also, you may want to change the style of **SPAN** so that when the user hovers the cursor over marked words, the cursor will change to a hand pointer, indicating that the user can click something. Put the **STYLE** element inside the **HEAD** element of your page.

```
<STYLE>
SPAN   {cursor:hand}
</STYLE>
```

Your Web page will look like Figure 11.12.

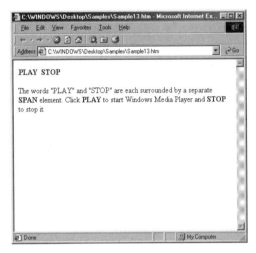

Figure 11.12 – *Creating a user interface with SPAN elements.*

Using DIV elements in a table

You can create custom user interfaces using art in a **TABLE** element. Each user interface element is enclosed by a **DIV** element so that it can be referenced by code easily. This can be very helpful if you are designing your Web page in a grid.

Create two pieces of art (called play.gif and stop.gif). Then insert them into the table using the **IMG** element. Surround each **IMG** element with a **DIV** element.

The code looks like the following:

```
<TABLE>
<TR>
    <TD>
        <DIV    onclick=StartMeUp()>
            <IMG   SRC="play.gif"   HEIGHT="35"   WIDTH="88"   BORDER="0">
        </DIV>
    </TD>
    <TD>
```

```
            <DIV    onclick=ShutMeDown()>
               <IMG   SRC="stop.gif"  HEIGHT="35"  WIDTH="88"  BORDER="0">
            </DIV>
         </TD>
      </TR>
      </TABLE>
```

The event handlers, **StartMeUp** and **ShutMeDown**, will be called when the **Play** and **Stop** buttons (represented by an arrow and a square) are clicked.

The Web page looks like Figure 11.13.

Figure 11.13 – *Artwork used as buttons in a table.*

Using DIV elements with absolute positioning

If you want a completely free-form layout, you can use **DIV** elements but define the absolute position of each art element by using the **style** attribute.

For example, the following code uses the same two art files but places them on the Web page in terms of the distance from the upper left corner in pixels.

```
<DIV    style="position:absolute;    top:100;    left:100;"    onclick=StartMeUp()>
<IMG   SRC="play.gif"  HEIGHT="35"  WIDTH="88"  BORDER="0"></DIV>

<DIV    style="position:absolute;    top:100;    left:200;"    onclick=ShutMeDown()>
<IMG   SRC="stop.gif"  HEIGHT="35"  WIDTH="88"  BORDER="0"></DIV>
```

The Web page would look like Figure 11.14.

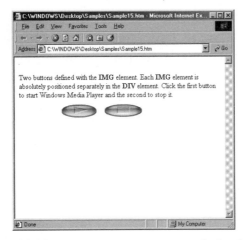

Figure 11.14 – *Two buttons positioned absolutely.*

Implementing event handlers

After you have inserted your **OBJECT** element and defined your user interface, all you have to do is write code for each function that is called by specific events. In the examples above, there are two events that you want handled. Each of them is a click event on a separate part of the user interface: one click for **Play** and another for **Stop**.

You can implement handlers in any language that Internet Explorer recognizes. The default scripting language for Internet Explorer is Microsoft JScript. You can use Microsoft Visual Basic Scripting Edition (VBScript) or other scripting languages, as long as Internet Explorer recognizes them.

The following is a simple JScript event handler for two buttons:

```
<SCRIPT>
<!--
function StartMeUp ()
{
    Player.URL  =  ".\\..\\media\\laure.wma";
}

function ShutMeDown ()
{
    Player.controls.stop();
}
-->
</SCRIPT>
```

227

The event handler code is enclosed in a **SCRIPT** element. Note that the handler code is also surrounded by the comment tags: "<!--" and "-->".

The handler code consists of two JScript functions, **StartMeUp** and **ShutMeDown**.

The **StartMeUp** function consists of setting a property of the Player object. The **Player** object is defined in the **OBJECT** element as "Player" and the property that is set is **URL**. The value is a file named laure.wma.

ShutMeDown is similar. It calls a method on the **Controls** object called **stop**. The **Controls** object cannot be called directly, and can only be accessed through the **control** property of the **Player** object.

Understanding Player control limitations

The Player ActiveX control does not contain all the functionality and features of Windows Media Player 7.

In particular, it does not have the following features:

- **Media Guide**
- **Radio Tuner**
- **Portable Device**
- **Skin Chooser**

The user interface for the **Media Library** feature is missing, but you can work with playlists and the media collection to create your own interfaces for a library of media.

In general, all the objects, methods, properties, and events that are covered in the Control Reference of the Windows Media Player 7 SDK can be implemented in a Web page.

Previous versions of the control

If you are familiar with previous versions of the Player control, four important things have changed.

- The **classid** attribute of the **OBJECT** element has changed. To get the core functionality of Player 7, you must use the new **classid**, "CLSID:6BF52A52-394A-11D3-B153-00C04F79FAA6".

- The new object model of the Player is very different. In the previous version, there was only one Player object, and all the methods, properties, and events were attached to it. The new model contains several objects, and some of them are contained inside other objects. The new object model is fully explained in the Windows Media Player 7 SDK.

- Several methods and properties have been removed. In the Windows Media Player 7 SDK, you can see a list of the properties and methods that have been removed.

- The ActiveX control for Windows Media Player 7 can only be used in a Web page. Previous versions of the control could be used in applications created with Microsoft Visual Basic and Visual C++.

Because of these changes, version 6.4 of the Windows Media Player ActiveX control is also installed with the new Player ActiveX control. If you use the old **classid** attribute in your OBJECT element, you can use the old Player in a Web page. Both versions are documented in the Windows Media Player 7 SDK, and you can use both versions simultaneously in a Web page if you give the **id** attributes different names and have the correct **classid** attributes for each version.

Ensuring that the Player is installed

Windows Media Player 7 must be installed on users' computers in order for them to get the full functionality of Web pages that have the Windows Media Player 7 embedded. To be sure that users know this, you can test to see whether Player 7 is installed. If it is not installed, you can then alert users and tell them where to get Windows Media Player 7.

You can use the following lines in your Web page code. Note that the **id** of the Player in the **OBJECT** tag is assumed to be "Player". If you name the object something else, substitute that name.

```
<SCRIPT    LANGUAGE="VBScript">
<!--
    'Run this code before anything else.
    'Note that it will set the URL property to a null string.
    'Do not set the URL property in a PARAM tag if you use this
    'code.

    'Allow the page to continue to process other code.
    'on error resume next

    'Create a message to tell the user to get Player 7.
    A="To take full advantage of this Web page, you must"
    B="download Microsoft(r) Windows Media(tm) Player 7 from the"
    C="Windows Media Web site at http://www.microsoft.com/windowsmedia"
    D="A + B + C"

    'Test if Player object is present and can use the URL property.
    WMP7=(Player.URL  =  "")

    'If the object is not present, alert the user by displaying the
    'message.
    if not (WMP7) then msgbox D

-->
</SCRIPT>
```

Going further

This chapter has given the simplest overview of using the Windows Media Player control in a Web page. Internet Explorer has many different technologies that can be used to create complex and very interactive user interfaces. There are dozens of books on using DHTML and ActiveX, and you can find out more at the MSDN Web Workshop at Microsoft's MSDN Web site:

http://msdn.microsoft.com/

The next chapter will show you how to create specialized audio and video that can be used in Web pages to make multimedia applications.

CHAPTER 12

Creating Custom Media Content

Windows Media Player provides four technologies that make media content more interactive. These technologies add data to existing audio and video files to allow the Player to control the media, integrate media with Web sites, provide greater Web page programmability, and include text with the visual and verbal content. The four technologies are:

Markers

You can add markers to an audio or video file to indicate a specific point in time. Markers can let users select a specific place they want to move the position of the media to, or you can use markers programmatically in skins or Web page scripts to change the media's current position.

URLs

Links to Web sites (known as *URLs*, or Uniform Resource Locators) can be embedded in content so that when the media file plays to a specified position, a Web page will be loaded. Embedding a URL in an audio or video stream is called *URL-flipping*, and provides a way to display Web pages that are synchronized with moving media.

Script commands

If you are creating complex skin or Web page scripts, you can add script commands to audio or video files that will be processed by your script as the media plays. You can create scripts that react to the content they receive.

Captioning

By using captioning, you can add text to audio and video content. Captioning can be used to provide text in situations where the audio cannot be heard, or you can provide text translations of audio in several different languages.

Each of these technologies uses different tools and techniques; the rest of the chapter will show you where and how to use each technology.

Using markers

A marker is a pointer to a specific location inside an audio or video file. Each marker has a name and a position. The position is a measure of time, in seconds, from the beginning of the file. A file can have any number of markers, but it can have only one marker at any given time position.

Inserting markers

You can insert markers into a file with the Windows Media Advanced Script Indexer tool, which is included on the companion CD of this book. It is also part of the Windows Media Resource Kit, which can be downloaded from the Windows Media Web site at:

> *http://www.microsoft.com/windowsmedia/*

Figure 12.1 shows the Advanced Script Indexer displaying three markers in a file named jeanne.wma. This file is included with the Windows Media Player 7 SDK.

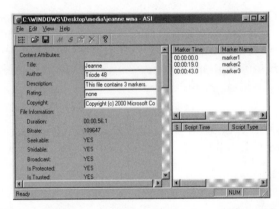

Figure 12.1 – *Advanced Script Indexer displaying a file with three markers.*

Marker names

The three markers in jeanne.wma are named marker1, marker2, and marker3. They could have any names as long as each name is unique. An application can listen for a marker name and respond when the marker is encountered in the specified file.

Marker times

The file jeanne.wma has a duration of 56.1 seconds. Markers are placed at the following points in the file:

- marker1: 0.0 seconds (the start of the file)

- marker2: 19.0 seconds

- marker3: 43.0 seconds

In this particular file, the markers are used to mark the opening, middle, and closing thematic portions of the music. But markers could be used for many different reasons. For example, you might want to divide a movie into scenes and allow users to switch to any scene they want at any time. Many DVD players allow this, making it possible for users to go back to named scenes. Moving to a specific position in a file is called *seeking*.

Using markers with the Player

Windows Media Player can work with files that have markers embedded in them. When you choose **File Markers** from the **View** menu, you are presented with a list of the named markers in the currently playing file.

Figure 12.2 shows the Player when it is ready for you to select a position in the file by choosing a marker. The thumb of the seek bar is on the left side, indicating that the song has just started.

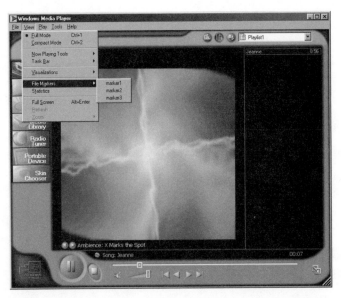

Figure 12.2 – *Getting ready to seek to a new position with a marker.*

When the third marker, marker3, is chosen, the Player moves the file position to 43 seconds into the song. Figure 12.3 shows the Player after the position has moved to the third marker.

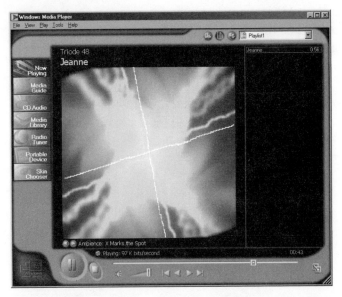

Figure 12.3 – *Position of the third marker in the file.*

Using markers in scripts

The following methods and properties are used with markers:

markerCount

You can use this property of the **Media** object to determine the number of markers in a file.

getMarkerName

This method of the **Media** object will give you the name of an indexed marker. For example, you could get the name of the third marker with getMarkerName(3).

getMarkerTime

This method of the **Media** object will give you the time of an indexed marker in seconds. For example, you can get the time of the second marker with getMarkerTime(2).

currentMarker

You can use this method of the **Controls** object to seek to the position of the indexed marker. For example, to seek to the position of the first marker in a file, you would write to **currentMarker**(1). You can also use **currentMarker** to read the position of the current marker. The current marker position extends from the position of the last marker encountered to just before the next marker.

The following JScript code shows how to use markers in script. The name of the **Player** object is **Player1** and the function **GoMarker** is called with the parameter of *mymark*, which is the marker number you want to seek to. This script is for use in a Web page. If you were using the script in a skin, the object name would be **player**.

```
function  GoMarker  (mymark)
{
    Player1.controls.currentMarker  =  mymark;
    MyText1.value  =  Player1.currentMedia.getMarkerName(mymark);
    MyText2.value  =  Player1.currentMedia.getMarkerTime(mymark);
    MyText3.value  =  Player1.currentMedia.markerCount;
}
```

The function reads a marker number and uses it to seek to the position of the numbered marker in a file. Then the marker name, marker time, and total number of markers in the file are copied and displayed in individual text boxes.

For more information about markers, see the Windows Media Player 7 SDK.

Using URLs

A URL (Uniform Resource Locator) is a link to a Web page. You can embed a URL in a media file or stream. When the URL is encountered by Windows Media Player, the Player will start Internet Explorer, which will display the Web page pointed to by the URL. You can use this feature to synchronize Web pages to specific points in your media content. For example, if you had a video narrating a trip to Egypt, you could have URLs embedded in the video that showed Web pages illustrating each portion of the lecture, just like a slide show.

A URL is a text string that provides a link to a document. The string must be in a format that uses a defined Web protocol such as *http* or *file*. A typical URL might be *http://www.microsoft.com/* or *file://c:\windows\desktop\myfile.doc*. There is no limit to the number of URLs you can embed in a file, but you can only have one URL at any given location. Using URLs in a media file is called *URL flipping*.

Inserting URLs

You can insert URLs into a media file with the Advanced Script Indexer tool, which is included on the companion CD of this book. It is also part of the Windows Media Resource Kit, which can be downloaded from the Windows Media Web site at:

> *http://www.microsoft.com/windowsmedia/*

Figure 12.4 shows the Advanced Script Indexer displaying three URLs in a file named glass.wmv. This file is included with the Windows Media Player 7 SDK.

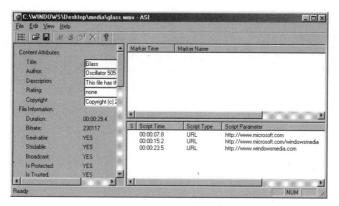

Figure 12.4 – *Advanced Script Indexer displaying a file with three URLs.*

The three URLs are links to the following locations:

- *http://www.microsoft.com/* (the main Microsoft Web site)

- *http://www.microsoft.com/windowsmedia/* (the main Windows Media Web site, where you can get information about Windows Media products and tools)

- *http://www.windowsmedia.com/* (the main WindowsMedia.com Web site, where you can go to get music, videos, and entertainment news)

URLs can be any text string that conforms to the Uniform Resource Identifier scheme as defined by the World Wide Web Consortium (W3C), the Internet standards committee. You can learn more about URLs at the W3C Web site:

http://www.w3.org/Addressing/

URL times

The video file glass.wmv is 29.4 seconds long. Three URLs are placed at the following points in the file:

- 7.8 seconds

- 15.2 seconds

- 23.5 seconds

Figure 12.5 shows Windows Media Player playing the glass.wmv file.

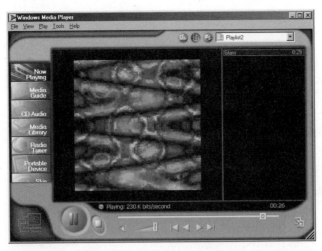

Figure 12.5 – *Video file with three URLs embedded in it.*

Note that this is an abstract video in the window, not a visualization.

When the Player encounters the first URL, it will display the main Microsoft Web site, as shown in Figure 12.6.

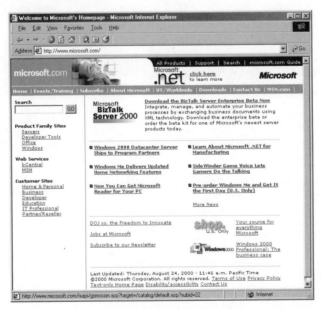

Figure 12.6 – *Web site displayed when the first URL is encountered in the glass.wmv file.*

Using URLs in scripts

You can use URL flipping in scripts to display Web pages. For example, you could write a script for a framed set of Web pages. One page could run the Player in one frame and display synchronized Web pages in the other frame.

The following methods and properties are used with URL flipping:

invokeURLs

You can use this property of the **Settings** object to determine whether URLs will be processed when they are encountered. The default value is True.

defaultFrame

This property is used to set the frame that the Web page will be displayed in.

The following JScript code shows how to use URL flipping in a framed set of Web pages. The page that defines the frame set uses the following HTML code:

```
<HTML>
<HEAD></HEAD>
<FRAMESET cols = "50%,50%">
    <FRAME src = "leftpage.htm" id = "left" name = "left">
    <FRAME src = "rightpage.htm" id = "right" name = "right">
</FRAMESET>
</HTML>
```

The page with the **id** of "left" contains the Player and is in the left frame. The page that contains the displayed URL has the **id** of "right" and is displayed on the right. Figure 12.7 shows the two Web pages surrounded by the frameset.

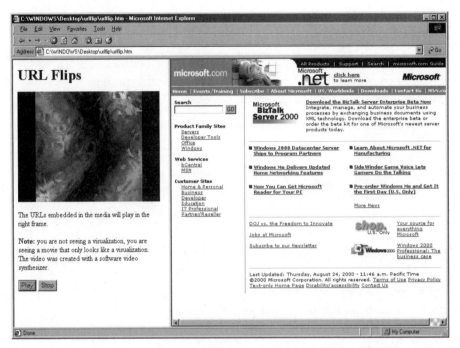

Figure 12.7 – *Frameset with the Player on the left and the Web site on the right.*

The left frame uses the following code to play and display the video.

```
<HTML>
<HEAD>
</HEAD>
<BODY>
<H1>URL   Flips</H1>
<OBJECT  ID = "Player1"
    CLASSID   =   "CLSID:6BF52A52-394A-11d3-B153-00C04F79FAA6">
    <PARAM NAME = "AutoStart" VALUE = "False">
    <PARAM NAME = "defaultFrame" VALUE = "right">
    <PARAM NAME = "UIMode" VALUE = "none">
</OBJECT>
<p>The URLs embedded in the media will play in the right frame.
<p><b>Note:</b> you are not seeing a visualization,
you are seeing a movie that only looks like a visualization. The video
was created with a software video synthesizer.</P>
<INPUT  TYPE="BUTTON"  NAME="BtnPlay"  VALUE="Play"  OnClick="StartMeUp()">
<INPUT  TYPE="BUTTON"  NAME="BtnStop"  VALUE="Stop"
OnClick="ShutMeDown()"><BR><BR>
<SCRIPT>
```

```
<!--
function StartMeUp ()
{
    Player1.URL = ".\\..\\media\\glass.wmv";
    Player1.controls.play();
}
function ShutMeDown ()
{
    Player1.controls.stop();
}
->
</SCRIPT>
</BODY>
</HTML>
```

Code very similar to the preceding is discussed in detail in Chapter 11. The **defaultFrame** property of the **Settings** object is initialized to the value of "right" by using the **PARAM** tag. This tells the Player to display any URLs in the frame with the **id** value of "right", which corresponds to the Web page on the right side of the frameset.

The HTML code for the Web page on the right side is a simple Web page with a default message. The body of the page will be replaced by the Web page called with the URL. The code looks like this:

```
<HTML>
<HEAD>
</HEAD>
<BODY>
<P>Watch this space!</P>
</BODY>
</HTML>
```

If a skin encounters a URL flip in the media it is playing, Internet Explorer will open and display the requested Web page. But the primary use of URL flips is in Web pages that use framesets, allowing you to create multimedia experiences in a browser.

Using script commands

Script commands are text strings that can be embedded in an audio or video file. When Windows Media Player encounters the commands, they generate unique events which a script can process to tie the content to the actions in a

Web page or skin. For example, you could change the color of a skin every time a different person began speaking in an video. The names for skin colors ("red", "blue", "green", and so on) could be embedded in the media to match the people speaking. When the media is processed by the Player, the color names could be used to change the skin color dynamically.

Inserting script commands

You can insert script commands into a media file with the Advanced Script Indexer tool, which is included on the companion CD of this book. It is also part of the Windows Media Resource Kit, which can be downloaded from the Windows Media Web site at:

http://www.microsoft.com/windowsmedia/

Figure 12.8 shows the Advanced Script Indexer displaying three script commands in a file named laure.wma.

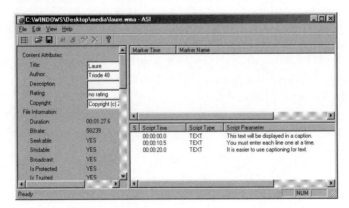

Figure 12.8 – *Advanced Script Indexer displaying a file with three script commands.*

If you play the file in the **Now Playing** view of the Player, you can see the text of the script commands in the **Captions** pane of the **Equalizer & Settings** pane. Figure 12.9 shows the Player displaying such a caption.

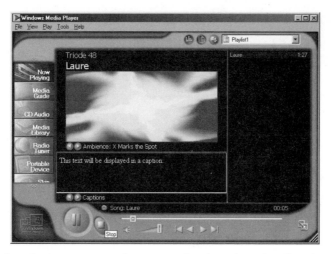

Figure 12.9 – *Script command caption displayed in the **Captions** pane of Now Playing.*

Script commands come in several types: URL, FILENAME, TEXT, EVENT, and OPENEVENT. Each script command has a specified time it will occur, a specified type, and a parameter that determines what will happen when the Player encounters the command. You can learn more about script commands in the Windows Media Player 7 SDK.

Custom script commands

In addition to the named script command types, you can specify custom script commands. They are similar to regular script commands, except that custom script commands can be completely open-ended. For example, you can create a command called **CustomScript** and give it parameters of **script1**, **script2**, and **script3**. Figure 12.10 shows an example of a custom command.

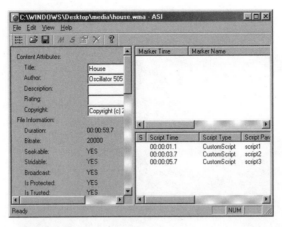

Figure 12.10 – *Custom script commands.*

Custom script commands can be extremely powerful when combined with the JScript **eval** method. You can send JScript keywords in the media stream that can be converted to JScript code you can compile with **eval** and run on the fly.

The Player automatically processes named script commands such as TEXT, URL, and so on. You can create a custom script command handler that will look for custom commands in the file or stream and process them when the Player encounters them.

The following code processes the custom commands given in Figure 12.10:

```
<SCRIPT   for="Player1"   event="scriptCommand(Type,   Param)"
LANGUAGE="JScript">
<!--
    var MyValue = 0;
    if (Type != "CustomScript")
        return;
    switch (Param) {
        case  "script1":
            MyValue = "red";
            break;
        case  "script2":
            MyValue = "green";
            break;
        case  "script3":
            MyValue = "blue";
            break;
        default:
            MyValue = "black";
```

```
    }
    MyFont.color  =  MyValue;
->
</Script>
```

This code is a standard JScript event handler that assumes the Player object name is "Player1". If the Type is not "CustomScript", the handler exits. Otherwise, it uses a switch statement to assign a color name to a variable based on the parameter value. The handler then assigns that color to a type font and exits.

You can use custom commands to trigger any custom event you want to design for a script in a Web page or a skin.

Using captioning

In the previous section you learned about a script command called TEXT that will display text in the **Captions** pane of the Player. By using a Windows Media metafile, you can display text from a separate text file instead of embedding each text string in the media itself. Metafiles have many uses in Windows Media technologies; you can learn more about them in the Windows Media Player 7 SDK.

For example, you can create a Web page that embeds the Player and displays a caption pane. See Figure 12.11 for an example of captioning.

Figure 12.11 – *Captioning in a Web page.*

The following code creates a Web page that uses captioning:

```html
<html>
<head>
    <title>Closed   Captioning   Example</title>
</head>
<body>
    <OBJECT    ID="Player1"    CLASSID="clsid:6BF52A52-394A-11d3-B153-00C04F79FAA6"
        height="200"    width="200">
            <param name="UIMode" value="none">
    </OBJECT>

        <table  height="100"  width="200"  border="3"  bordercolor="blue">
            <tr  align="center">
                <td bgcolor="white">
                    <font  color="blue"  size="2">Captioning</font></td>
            </tr>
            <tr  height="75">
                <td  bgcolor="blue"><div  id="CapText"></div></td>
            </tr>
        </table>
<BR>
        <INPUT  TYPE="BUTTON"  NAME="BtnPlay"  VALUE="Play"  OnClick="StartMeUp()">
        <INPUT  TYPE="BUTTON"  NAME="BtnStop"  VALUE="Stop"  OnClick="ShutMeDown()">

<SCRIPT>
<!--

function   StartMeUp  ()
{
        Player1.closedCaption.CaptioningID  =  "CapText"
         Player1.closedCaption.SAMIFileName  =  ".\\..\\media\\ccsample.smi"
        Player1.URL  =  ".\\..\\media\\seattle.wmv";
        Player1.controls.play();
}

function   ShutMeDown  ()
{
        Player1.controls.stop();
}

->
</SCRIPT>
</body>
</html>
```

The video and caption display areas are created with a table. A blue table cell contains a **DIV** element with an **ID** of CapText. The cell is used by the **captioningID** property of the **Captioning** object to define where the captioning text will be displayed. The **SAMIFileName** property defines the location of the Synchronized Accessible Media Interchange (SAMI) file. The URLs use a relative path for both files and require extra backslashes for escapement. The UI mode is given the value of "none" in a **PARAM** element so that the UI controls will not be displayed.

Captioning uses the SAMI file format with the file extension .smi. For more information about SAMI, see the Microsoft Web site at:

http://www.microsoft.com/enable/sami/

The file that contains the captioning information, ccsample.smi, must be in the same directory as the file it captions. The file looks like this:

```
<SAMI>
<HEAD>
    <Title>Close  Captioning  Sample</Title>

        <STYLE   TYPE="text/css">
          <!--
            P  {margin-top:3pt;  margin-left:5pt;  font-size:  10pt;
                font-family:  tahoma,  sans-serif;  font-weight:  normal;
                color:  white;}
            .ENUSCC  {Name:'English  Captions'  lang:  en-US;  SAMIType:CC;}
          -->
        </Style>
</HEAD>

<BODY>
    <SYNC   Start=1000>
        <P  Class=ENUSCC>Great  reasons  to  visit  Seattle,  brought  to  you  by
two  out-of-staters.
    <SYNC   Start=4000>
        <P  Class=ENUSCC>So  you  know,  there  are  lots  of  great  reasons  to  come
visit  Seattle.
    <SYNC   Start=7000>
        <P  Class=ENUSCC>That's  right,  I  came  here  because  of  the  coffee.
    <SYNC   Start=9000>
        <P  Class=ENUSCC>Yah,  everyone  knows  the  coffee.
    <SYNC   Start=12000>
        <P  Class=ENUSCC>And  I  heard  about  the  drivers.
```

```
        <SYNC   Start=14000>
            <P  Class=ENUSCC>Well,  you  know,  but  then  it  rains...and  it's  bad,
    it's  bad.
        <SYNC   Start=19000>
            <P  Class=ENUSCC>But  the  traffic  in  general  is...
        <SYNC   Start=21000>
            <P   Class=ENUSCC>Terrible.
        <SYNC   Start=23000>
            <P  Class=ENUSCC>OK,  yah,  yah.   But,  the  weather!
        <SYNC   Start=26500>
            <P  Class=ENUSCC>It  doesn't  rain  all  the  time...yes,  it  does.
        <SYNC   Start=30000>
            <P  Class=ENUSCC>Yah.    Never  mind.
        <SYNC   Start=34000>
            <P  Class=ENUSCC>End  of  Stream.
    </BODY>
    </SAMI>
```

Markers, URL flips, script commands, and captioning are powerful tools for creating interactive media files. You can learn more about them in the Windows Media Player 7 SDK on the companion CD.

CHAPTER 13

Creating Multimedia Applications

In addition to the skin technology you read about in Part 2 of this book, Windows Media Player provides a new technology called content borders. Borders enable you to package audio and video with a modified skin to create a complete multimedia application.

Using borders

Borders use the skin technology in a different way. An ordinary skin only *plays* media, but a border *includes* the media. Borders are a set of files that combine artwork with audio and video. A typical border will include one or more audio and video files and all the files needed to display the artwork.

The biggest difference between a skin and a border is that the skin has the capability of playing a limitless variety of audio and video, whereas a border is programmed to play only a fixed selection of audio and video. A border is more like a music album with a set number of songs; a skin is more like a radio with a vast, ever-changing set of songs. Borders have the advantage of being able to create prepackaged units of information for advertising or multimedia entertainment.

The following figures will show the visual difference between a skin and a border. The differences are in where they are displayed and whether they have media included. These comparison figures will show you how and where a border is displayed and demonstrate that a skin can be converted into a border.

Figure 13.1 shows a hypothetical skin that could be created from the Windows Media Technologies 7 logo.

Figure 13.1 – *Hypothetical skin created from the Windows Media Technologies 7 logo.*

The skin in Figure 13.1 replaces the user interface of the Player.

A border, however, puts the visual image in the left pane of the **Now Playing** view of the full mode Player. This portion of the Player is the area that displays visualizations and videos. A border can only appear in this left pane. Even if the playlist pane is hidden, the border will be displayed lined up on the left edge of the pane.

Figure 13.2 shows the same hypothetical skin being displayed in the left pane of the **Now Playing** view of the full mode Player.

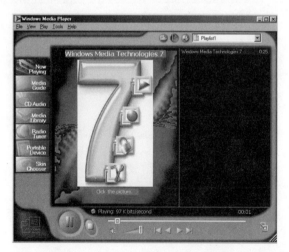

Figure 13.2 – *Hypothetical border displayed in the* ***Now Playing*** *view.*

The border contains the artwork of the logo, but also contains the functionality of a skin. You can create buttons and sliders for a border that control the functions of the Player. A border has two main differences from a skin:

- A border is displayed in the left pane of the **Now Playing** view in the full mode of Windows Media Player. It does not replace the user interface of the full mode Player, but a border can duplicate or enhance Player functionality.

- A border can contain media clips. In the hypothetical example above, the border contains a 25 second song called *Windows Media Technologies 7*. The ability to include content allows the creation of multimedia applications. This combination of media content and border art creates a unique, fixed package. This fixed content cannot be changed or modified the way that media available through skins can.

By using the programming power of skins and the media handling capabilities of the Player, you can combine audio, video, artwork, and interactive programming. The example skin above also contains a link to a Web site. If you "click the picture" as requested, Internet Explorer will start up and display the main Windows Media Web site.

The fact that borders are complete packages of fixed media selections means you can do amazing things. Here are a few ideas to think about for border applications:

- You can create advertisements by associating a border skin with specific content. For example, if you had a record company, you could create a Windows Media Download (WMD) file with sample songs from several CDs. Each song could load a skin that shows an image of the CD cover art. When the user clicked the cover art in the border, a Web page about that album could be launched. You could include the WMD file on every music CD you distribute, using the Enhanced Music CD format or another format that combines CD tracks with computer programs.

- You can create educational programming with a branching sequence of instructional video clips. You could show the first clip, display a question on your border, and let the student click a button. If they gave a right answer, the next clip would show. If they gave a wrong answer, another clip could display that would explain more about the subject. The clips and the software would all be inside one WMD file.

- You can create computer music by including several small files playing different notes on a scale and letting the user click buttons to create instant musical compositions. By using markers and seeking, you could also create musical instruments using a single large file.

How to create borders

If you know how to create a skin, you can create a border. Essentially all you do is create a skin, assemble your media content, and compress the skin and content together into a new file.

> **Note** Because the border file package has a different file name extension, the skin inside it will no longer be treated as a skin. It becomes a border and its functionality is limited to what a border has been specified to do.

Follow these steps to create a border and package it.

Create a skin
You must first create a skin. The skin must contain the skin definition file, one or more art files, and any JScript files. The skin must then be compressed and given the .wmz file name extension.

Assemble your content
Put all the files that you want to use into a folder. You can include any type of audio or video files that the Player can play.

Write a Windows Media metafile
The Player won't know which skin to load unless you create a Windows Media metafile that uses the **SKIN** element. The metafile can also be used to create a playlist that describes the content included in the package.

Create the package
Compress the skin, content, and metafile together into a new file with the .wmd file name extension. When the Player loads the WMD file, a border will be displayed and the content will start playing.

Details about each step are given below.

Creating a skin

Anything you want to do in a skin, you can probably do in a border. You can add buttons, sliders, text, and more.

In terms of skin coding, there are a few limitations to borders:

- There are a few functions that aren't appropriate for borders. For example, using the **Return to Full Mode** functionality wouldn't be useful because the Player is already in full mode.

- If you want to display a known visualization or a video, you will need to create an area on your skin to display them using the **EFFECT** or **VIDEO** elements. If your border is smaller than the display area, a visualization can be playing in the background. Figure 13.2 shows a visualization displaying behind the border art.

- Because the border is displayed inside the left pane of the **Now Playing** view of the full mode Player, the border edges may be clipped if the full mode Player is resized. As a skin creator, you can't tell in advance how large the display area for your border will be. Figure 13.3 shows an example of a border being clipped after the Player was resized. Because the playlist pane can be resized, the minimum size of the border display is approximately 210 pixels wide and 220 pixels high. You may want to keep your pixels this height.

Figure 13.3 – *Resized Player in full mode clipping part of the border image.*

Note that if you change the view to compact mode while you are playing a border, the border will change to a skin. The border artwork for the above skin is displayed in a square defined by the height and width of the skin, and looks like Figure 13.4.

Figure 13.4 – *Border playing in compact mode.*

Using borders in compact mode may produce unexpected results. You may want to test your borders to see what they do if the user changes the view to compact mode.

Assembling the content

Choose the audio and video files you want to include with your package. Anything that the Player can play, you can include.

If you are creating multimedia applications, you may want to investigate the possibilities of using specialized content such as markers, URLs, and script commands. You can find out more about specialized content in Chapter 12.

Writing the metafile

You need to create a Windows Media metafile to make your border work. A Windows Media metafile is a text file with the file name extension of .asx. Metafiles have many uses in Windows Media Technology, but this chapter focuses on their use as the packing list for borders. You can learn more about Windows Media metafiles in the Windows Media Player 7 SDK.

Every border must have a metafile that uses the **SKIN** element to define which skin will be loaded. Metafiles use XML code that contains elements and attributes.

The following code can be used to create a metafile for a border that will use a skin called package.wmz.

```
<asx version = "3.0">
<title> Musical Clips </title>
<skin href = "package.wmz" />
```

Every metafile must start out with the first line identifying the metafile version. The **TITLE** elements are then used to identify the title for the information that follows. In this case, the information will be a playlist and the **TITLE** element will define the title of the playlist. You must then use the **href** attribute of **SKIN** to define the location of the skin file you want to use for the border.

You can also use the same metafile to create a playlist that can be used to identify your content. Here is a playlist for three songs, using the metafile tags as defined in the SDK.

```
<entry>
    <title>  Guitar  clip  </title>
    <ref    href="guitar.wma"/>
</entry>

<entry>
    <title>  Banjo  clip  </title>
    <ref    href="banjo.wma"/>
</entry>

<entry>
    <title>  Synthesizer  clip  </title>
    <ref    href="synth.wma"/>
</entry>
```

Figure 13.5 shows a border that uses the preceding metafile to create the border as well as the playlist for the content that was packaged with the border.

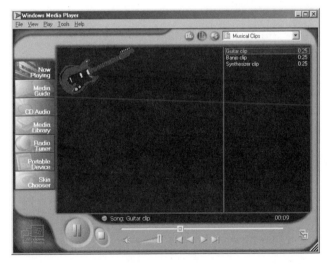

Figure 13.5 – *Border packaged with three songs defined by a playlist.*

Putting the package together

When you have all the pieces, you are ready to create the final border package. Use this checklist to make sure you have everything.

- Make sure you have a working skin. The compressed skin file must contain the skin definition file, all art files needed for the skin, and any

JScript files. The file name extension must be .wmz and you can only have one skin file.

- Make sure you have the content you want to include and that every file is playable by the Windows Media Player. You can have as many files as you want.

- Make sure you have a Windows Media metafile that includes a **SKIN** element with an **href** attribute that points to the skin you want to use. The metafile can also contain entries that define the order, titles, and file names of each content file you want to include. There is only one metafile and the extension should be .asx.

When you have the three types of files (skin, content, metafile) ready to go, compress them together into one single file. This file should have the file name extension of .wmd. Your package is ready for distribution.

Creating a sample border

The following code will create a simple border. Use these steps:

1. Create a skin.

2. Assemble the content.

3. Write the metafile.

4. Put the package together.

Creating a sample skin

The skin for this example will not have any artwork. Instead, a visualization will be used to create a visual image.

The skin definition file will look like this:

```
<THEME>
    <VIEW
        titleBar="false">
    <EFFECTS
        visible="true"
        windowed="false"
        height="400"
        width="400"
        currentEffectType="ambience"/>
    </VIEW>
</THEME>
```

This code sets up a simple view with no title bar. Then a visualization is created with the **EFFECTS** element that is visible but not windowed. A height and width of 400 pixels is set up to make sure the visualization fills the area of the border. The visualization that will be used is called "ambience".

The skin definition file for this skin is a text file named package.wms. When compressed, it is named package.wmz.

Assembling the content

The content for this sample will be three short musical files:

• Guitar.wma

• Banjo.wma

• Synth.wma

These songs are included with the samples for the Windows Media Player 7 SDK.

Writing the metafile

The metafile for the border will look like this:

```
<asx version = "3.0">
<title> Musical Clips </title>
<skin href = "package.wmz"/>

<entry>
    <title> Guitar clip </title>
    <ref    href="guitar.wma"/>
</entry>

<entry>
    <title> Banjo clip </title>
    <ref    href="banjo.wma"/>
</entry>

<entry>
    <title> Synthesizer clip </title>
    <ref    href="synth.wma"/>
</entry>

</asx>
```

This creates a metafile that will be a playlist named "Musical Clips". The metafile file name is package.asx. The href attribute of the **SKIN** element defines the skin that will be used as "package.wmz". Three playlist entries are defined for the three musical clips.

Putting the package together

The following files are compressed together into one package:

- Package.wmz

- Guitar.wma

- Banjo.wma

- Synth.wma

- Package.asx

The name of the compressed package is package.wmd.

When you double-click the file, the Player will load it and will look like Figure 13.6.

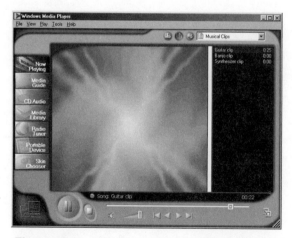

Figure 13.6 – *Sample border with three files.*

CHAPTER 14

Creating Custom Visualizations

This chapter will show you how to create a custom visualization. You will learn the software tools you need to use, the coding template you will work with, and the programming interfaces you will need to implement. A simple visualization will be discussed in detail.

> **Note** The material covered in this chapter requires a basic understanding of C++ and Windows programming. Only an overview of visualization programming is given here, and you should consult the Windows Media Player 7 SDK that is on the companion CD of this book for detailed information.

Chapter 1 discussed how to install and use visualizations from the end-user point of view. From the developer's point of view, visualizations are software programs that take audio data provided by Windows Media Player and convert it to visual images for display by the Player. The audio data from the Player is updated several times a second and so is the display. The result is an animated frame-by-frame movie of rapidly changing images that are synchronized to the music.

Software tools

You will need the following tools to create visualizations:

Microsoft Visual C++ 5.0
You will use this to compile the code you write into your visualization. You must have version 5.0 or later. The code for your visualization must be written in C++.

Windows Media Player 7 SDK
This SDK includes a tool called the Windows Media Player Custom Visualization Wizard. You will need the wizard to create the supporting code for your visualization. The SDK also includes complete information on every aspect of creating a visualization.

Microsoft Windows Platform SDK

You will need this SDK to understand the programming interfaces of
Microsoft Windows, especially the Graphics Display Interface (GDI).
Your visualization is a Windows DLL (dynamic-link library). You will
also need to understand the Component Object Model (COM) because
visualizations are COM controls.

Windows Media Player 7

If you don't have Windows Media Player 7, you won't be able to test
your visualization. You may also want to study the visualizations that
others have created and understand the ways that a particular
visualization is affected through presets and properties.

Installing Visual C++

Be sure you install Microsoft Visual C++ 5.0 or later. Follow the installation
instructions that come with the compiler. You will want to include the MSDN
Help documentation because it will include the Microsoft Platform SDK for
32-bit Windows.

Installing the Windows Media Player 7 SDK

A copy of the Windows Media Player 7 SDK is included on the companion
CD that comes with this book. Install it on the same computer you will be using to develop your visualizations. You will need the wizard that comes with
the SDK, but you will also want to read the documentation that covers visualizations.

Installing the Visualization Wizard

After you have installed Visual C++ and the Windows Media Player 7 SDK,
you are ready to install the Windows Media Player Visualization Wizard. It
will be installed on your computer in a subfolder of the folder you chose to
install the Windows Media Player 7 SDK in. The subfolder will be:

```
wmpsdk\wizards\viz
```

where *wmpsdk* is the name of the folder you chose to install the SDK in. If
you can't remember where you installed the SDK, you can search for the file
named WMEffect.awx.

The file WMEffect.awx is a Visual C++ wizard that generates the minimum source code needed to create a visualization. To use it, you must copy it to a folder that is used by Visual C++ to store the COM wizards it uses. This folder may vary depending on how you installed Visual C++, as well as what operating system you installed it on. You can copy the wizard to:

```
SystemDrive\Program    Files\Microsoft    Visual    Studio\Common\MSDev98\Bin\IDE
```

where *SystemDrive* is the drive you installed Visual C++ on. You can also use:

```
SystemDrive\Program    Files\Microsoft    Visual    Studio\Common\MSDev98\Template
```

If you're not sure where to put the wizard, search for files with the extension .awx. Visual C++ comes with several default wizards that will be in the same folder.

Confirming the installation of the wizard

You can be sure you have installed the wizard properly by using the following procedure:

Start Visual C++ and click **New** on the **File** menu. You will see a dialog box that looks like Figure 14.1.

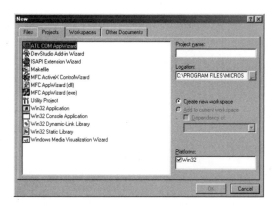

Figure 14.1 – *Projects tab of the New dialog box.*

Be sure you click the **Projects** tab of the dialog box. You should see a list of project types and wizards. You should see a project called "Windows Media Visualization Wizard". If you don't see it, the wizard isn't in the right folder.

After you have made sure that the wizard is installed, you can create a new project any time by selecting the wizard, typing a project name in the **Project name** box, and clicking the **OK** button.

Installing Windows Media Player 7

You should install Windows Media Player 7 before you build your visualization. Part of the build process will involve running and testing your visualization, and if you don't have the Player installed, your visualization won't work. Visualizations will not work on earlier versions of the Player.

Creating your project templates

Because visualizations are COM controls, it would be very difficult to create a visualization from scratch. Creating a COM control requires a complete understanding of the underlying framework of COM. For this reason, a COM wizard is provided that will create all the code you need to build a fully working visualization. The wizard will create several files and implement the minimum code to create a simple visualization with two presets. You can use these files as a template to create your own visualization. You will not need to change most of the files that the wizard creates, only ones that affect your visualization directly.

Project files

The wizard will create the following files for your project:

effects.idl
> The IDL (Interface Definition Language) file for all visualizations. You will probably not want to change this file.

project.cpp
> The main project file for the methods that will be called from the Player. Default code is supplied by the wizard. You must change the code to create your own custom visualization.

projectdll.cpp
> The code for setting up the DLL (dynamic-link library). You will probably not want to change this file.

projectdll.def

The definition file for the DLL. You will probably not want to change this file.

projectdll.rc

The resource file for the DLL. You may want to change this file if you add, subtract, or modify preset strings. If you need to add other resources, add them here.

iproject.idl

The IDL file for your project. You will probably not want to change this file.

StdAfx.cpp

The **#include** files for MFC (Microsoft Foundation Classes). You will probably not want to change this file.

project.h

The header file for your project. Declarations for your project go here. If you add, subtract, or modify presets, you will want to change this file. You can also add your own declarations here.

resource.h

The header file for resources. If you add, subtract, or modify presets, you will want to change this file.

StdAfx.h

The header file for MFC **#include** details. You will probably not want to change this file.

project.rgs

The registry file for your project. Use this to register your project in the Microsoft Windows Registry.

project.wms

A Windows Media Player skin definition file. You can use this to test your finished visualization.

basetsd.h

Definitions for data types. You probably do not want to modify this file.

effects.h

Header file for all visualizations. You probably do not want to modify this file.

iproject.h

Header file for the project IDL. Generated by the build.

iproject.tlb

Type Library (TLB) file for the project. Generated by the build.

iproject_i.idl

MIDL (Microsoft Interface Definition Language) file for your project. Generated by the build.

Creating the files

When you are ready to create your first project, start Visual C++ and click **New** on the **File** menu. You should see a dialog box similar to Figure 14.1.

Select the Windows Media Visualization Wizard in the list of project types and type the name of the project you want to create in the **Project name** box. A project named "MyFirstViz" is shown in Figure 14.2.

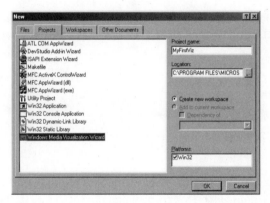

Figure 14.2 – *Visualization project named "MyFirstViz" ready to be created.*

You will see a confirmation dialog box that displays all the information about your new project. Figure 14.3 shows a confirmation dialog box for the "MyFirstViz" project.

Figure 14.3 – *Project confirmation dialog box for the "MyFirstViz" project.*

If you click OK, the project will be created. Visual C++ will look like Figure 14.4.

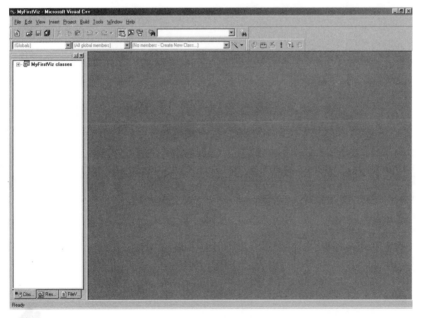

Figure 14.4 – *Visual C++ with the new project ready for coding.*

If you click **FileView** at the bottom left and expand the folders, you can see all the files that have been created for your new project. Figure 14.5 shows the files.

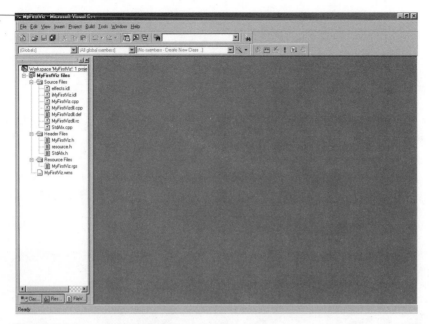

Figure 14.5 – *View of the files that have been created by the wizard.*

Building a test visualization

The files that were installed contain the complete code for a simple visualization. You can build a test visualization now. Be sure that Windows Media Player 7 is also installed on the same computer before you build.

Click **Rebuild All** on the **Build** menu. The compilation will start and you will see messages scrolling by in the Build window at the bottom of the screen. When the build is finished, you should see the following message:

```
MyFirstViz.dll - 0 error(s), 0 warning(s)
```

If you choose another project name, the DLL file name will be the project name with a .dll file name extension. Figure 14.6 shows the completed "MyFirstViz" project build.

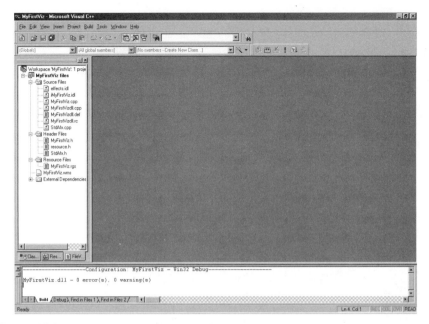

Figure 14.6 – *Completion of the build process with no errors or warnings.*

Seeing the test visualization

You can see the visualization that was created by starting Windows Media Player. Your visualization name will be the same as the project name. Figure 14.7 shows the Player with the first preset of your visualization.

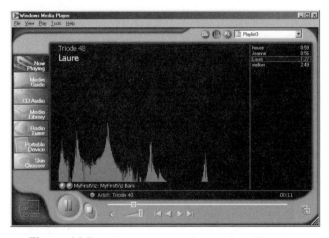

Figure 14.7 – *First preset of test visualization.*

If you do not see the visualization you created, play an audio file and click the **Next Visualization** button until you see something that looks like Figure 14.7. The visualization name is the name to the left of the colon in the visualization name display. In this case it is "MyFirstViz". The preset name is the name to the right of the colon. In this case it is "MyFirstViz Bars". You can change the name of the visualization and its presets in your code. Presets allow you to create more than one visualization in a single DLL. Each of the presets can be different, but they share a common code base.

Figure 14.8 shows the other preset for the test visualization.

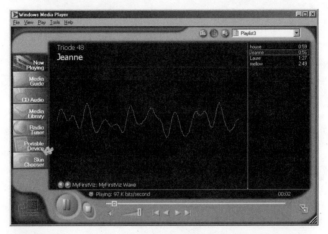

Figure 14.8 – *Second preset of the test visualization.*

The Visualization Wizard also creates a simple skin using the same name as the project but with the file name extension .wms. This skin can be used to show you the visualization type, visualization title, preset number and preset title. Figure 14.9 shows the skin that the wizard builds.

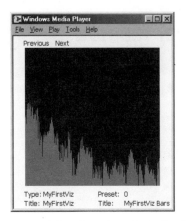

Figure 14.9 – *Skin created by the wizard to display visualizations.*

Implementing the Render interface

Windows Media Player sends information to your visualization at frequent intervals. You must write code that responds to that information every time the Player sends it. The **Render** method is where that code must reside.

Control flow between Player and visualization

Here is the sequence of interaction between the Player and your visualization:

1. At a timed interval, Windows Media Player takes a snapshot of the audio that is playing. The exact timing will depend on the media being played.

2. Windows Media Player supplies the data from that snapshot to your visualization through the **Render** method.

3. You must write code that will run when **Render** is called. Your code draws in a window defined by Windows Media Player.

4. Windows Media Player displays what your code drew.

5. This process repeats several times a second, creating graphical animations that are timed to the music.

Parameters of the Render method

The **Render** method looks like this:

```
STDMETHODIMP CMyFirstViz::Render(TimedLevel *pLevels, HDC hdc, RECT *prc)
{
}
```

The parameters supply the following information to the code that you will create:

TimedLevel

This is a structure that defines the audio data your code will be analyzing. The structure is composed of two arrays. The first array is based on frequency information and contains a snapshot of the audio spectrum divided into 1024 portions. Each cell of the array contains a value from 0 to 255. The first cell starts at 20 Hz and the last at 22050 Hz. The array is two dimensional to represent stereo audio. The second array is based on waveform information and corresponds to audio power, where stronger waves have larger values. The waveform array is a granular snapshot of the last 1024 slices of audio power taken at very small time intervals. This array also is two dimensional to represent stereo audio.

HDC

This is a Microsoft Windows handle to a device context. This provides a way to identify the drawing surface to Windows. You do not need to create it, you just need to use it for specific drawing function calls.

RECT

This is a Microsoft Windows rectangle that defines the size of a drawing surface. This is a simple rectangle with four properties: **left**, **right**, **top**, and **bottom**. The actual values are supplied by Windows Media Player so that you can determine how the user or skin developer has sized the window you will draw on. It also determines the position on the HDC that the effect is supposed to render on.

For more details about each parameter, see the Windows Media Player 7 SDK.

Implementing presets

Presets are provided as a way to create different effects with by the same visualization. For example, you could create a glow effect that was generated by one block of code, but use a preset to determine the color of the glow. Your preset names might be Red, Green, and Blue.

The Visualization Wizard defines two presets for the code it generates. One is called Bars and the other is called Wave. The Bars preset displays bars that show the activity in the audio spectrum, and use the waveform data. The Wave preset displays a wiggling line that shows the audio power of the waveform.

You should change the default presets of Bars and Wave. To do this, you must change code in the **Render** method and the **GetPresetTitle** method of the default code generated by the wizard. You also need to change information in the preset enumeration, preset header, and preset string resource if you add, subtract, or change presets.

Render method

The **IWMPEffects::Render** method is in the file *projectname*.cpp, where *projectname* is the project name you chose when you ran the wizard.

The generated code in the **Render** method uses a switch statement to choose between two presets. The current preset is whatever the user selects in Windows Media Player. If you want to change which code runs for a particular preset or add or subtract a preset, modify the switch statement accordingly.

The two presets are defined by the **PRESET_BARS** and **PRESET_SCOPE** enumerations. The choice of which preset will be called is defined by **m_nPreset**.

The **Render** method is where the main portions of the code you implement will reside.

GetPresetTitle

The **IWMPEffects::GetPresetTitle** method is in the file *projectname*.cpp, where *projectname* is the project name you chose when you ran the wizard.

The **GetPresetTitle** method sets up the relationships between the preset enumerations and the string resources. The enumerations **PRESET_BARS** and

PRESET_SCOPE are generated by the wizard and use the string resources **IDS_BARSPRESETNAME** and **IDS_SCOPEPRESETNAME**.

Preset Enumeration

The preset enumeration is defined in the file *projectname*.h, where *projectname* is the project name you chose when you ran the wizard.

The enumeration defines the current two presets and the count. If you add or subtract presets or change the enumeration, be sure you change this enumeration so that the count and order of presets is correct. This enumeration is used to make sure that you call the correct preset in the **Render method**.

Resource Header

You must set the resources for names of your preset in the resource.h header file. The current presets are defined as:

```
#define IDS_BARSPRESETNAME        102
#define IDS_SCOPEPRESETNAME       103
```

If you add or subtract presets, you must change the resource header and the numbers for them.

Resource Strings

The actual names of the presets are defined in the resource file *projectname*dll.rc, where *projectname* is the project name you chose when you ran the wizard. You can edit this file by hand or use the resource editor included with Microsoft Visual C++.

The preset names generated are the name of the visualization plus the specific preset. The resource file for the generated code will define them as:

```
IDS_BARSPRESETNAME        "projectname Bars"
IDS_SCOPEPRESETNAME       "projectname Wave"
```

where *projectname* is the name of the project name you chose when you ran the wizard. This is where you will change the actual names of the presets and this is how they will be referred to and displayed by Windows Media Player.

Sample code

The following visualization code will draw an alien eye that blinks open and closed according to the frequency and volume of the music. The code is written in blocks that perform the following tasks:

1. A black background is painted to create a canvas.

2. A loop is set up to walk through the array of waveform and frequency information.

3. If the frequency value of a particular cell is too low, the cell is skipped.

4. Pens and brushes for the eye are created.

5. The width and height of the eye are calculated based on the cell data.

6. The ellipse is drawn.

7. The pens and brushes for the eye are destroyed.

8. After the loop is finished, the background brush is deleted.

Here is the code to create this sample visualization:

```
// Fill background with black.
// Create a black brush.
HBRUSH hBackBrush = ::CreateSolidBrush( 0 );
// Fill background rectangle with brush.
::FillRect( hdc, prc, hBackBrush );

// Walk through the array current values..
// Buffer is currently 1024 cells.
for (int i = 0; i < (SA_BUFFER_SIZE - 1) ; ++i)
    {

    // If frequency value too low, exit loop.
    int mytest = pLevels->frequency[0][i];
    if (mytest < 10)
        {
        i = i + 1;
        break;
        }

    // Create foreground pen.
    // Create solid red 3 pixel pen.
    HPEN hNewPen     = ::CreatePen( PS_SOLID, 3, 0xFF );
```

```
    // Add the pen to the device context.
    HPEN  hOldPen= static_cast<HPEN>(::SelectObject(  hdc,  hNewPen ));

    // Create foreground brush.
    COLORREF  frontcolor;
    frontcolor = RGB( 0, 0xFF, 0);          // Make it green.
    // Create the brush.
    HBRUSH  hFrontBrush = ::CreateSolidBrush( frontcolor );
    ::SelectObject(hdc,hFrontBrush);        // Add it to the DC.

    // Get current array data
    // Power value of cell..
    int  y = pLevels->waveform[0][i];
    // Frequency value of cell.
    int  x = pLevels->frequency[0][i];

    int myleft = prc->left + x;
    int mytop = prc->top + y;
    int myright = prc->right - x;
    int mybottom = prc->bottom -y;

    // Display the ellipse.
    ::Ellipse(hdc,  myleft,  mytop,  myright,  mybottom);

    // Delete foreground pen.
    if (hNewPen)
        {
        ::SelectObject(  hdc,  hOldPen );
        ::DeleteObject(  hNewPen );
        }
    // Delete foreground brush.
    if (hFrontBrush)
        {
        ::DeleteObject(  hFrontBrush );
        }

    }
// Delete background brush.
if (hBackBrush)
    {
    ::DeleteObject(  hBackBrush );
    }
```

Figure 14.10 shows the sample visualization with the alien eye open.

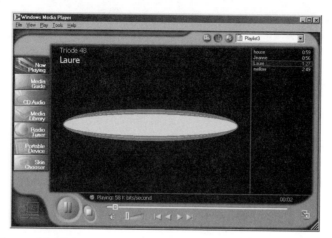

Figure 14.10 – *Sample visualization with alien eye open.*

The shape of the eye changes height and width several times a second, giving the appearance of opening and shutting. Figure 14.11 shows the alien eye shutting.

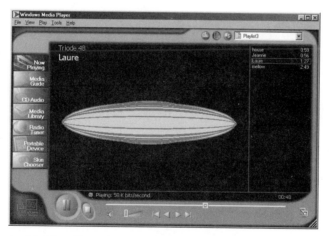

Figure 14.11 – *Sample visualization with alien eye shutting.*

Going further

This chapter only scratches the surface of how to create visualizations. You can find out more details in the Windows Media Player 7 SDK which is on the companion CD of this book. In addition, you may want to read the following two books from Microsoft Press:

Programming Windows, by Charles Petzold

Inside OLE, by Kraig Brockschmidt

The first book will help you to understand Windows Programming; the chapters on GDI will be very helpful for creating visualizations. The second book will help you to understand more about COM and how the visualization control code is put together.

After you have created a visualization, you can submit it to the Visualization Gallery at the WindowsMedia.com Web site. See the Windows Media Player 7 SDK for more information on preparing and submitting visualizations.

Visualizations are relatively easy to write if you are an experienced Windows programmer. The GDI technology is well-documented and has been in use for many years. You can draw on the screen to make eye-catching art with points, lines, and shapes. Windows Media Player will take care of the difficult tasks of screen buffering and synchronizing the animation to the music, letting you focus on creating art that will entertain a wide audience. The only limit is you imagination.

This book provides a brief tour of the features and programming capabilities of Windows Media Player 7. While it only begins to describe all the powerful functionality beneath the surface, I hope it gives you some insight into some of the many useful and fascinating things you can do with the Player. Most of all, I hope it inspires you to develop your own unique skins and visualizations, and gives you innovative ideas for creating and playing multimedia content. I hope you enjoy reading this book as much as I enjoyed writing it.

Glossary

This glossary defines terms used in *Windows Media Player 7 Handbook*. In addition to Windows Media Player terms, Microsoft Windows Media Technologies and other common industry terms are also defined.

A

.aiff

> A Macintosh AIFF file. *See also* media formats.

.asf

> A Windows Media file. Advanced streaming format. *See also* media formats.

.asx

> A Windows Media file. Advanced stream redirector. *See also* media formats.

.au

> A UNIX audio file. *See also* media formats.

.avi

> A Windows multimedia video file. *See also* media formats.

ambient

> In the context of Windows Media Player skin creation, an ambient attribute or event is one that applies to all or most of the skin elements documented in the SDK.

analog

> Traditional format in which audio and video are transmitted using a wave or analog signal.

anchor window

> A small window that appears in the lower right corner of the screen when Windows Media Player is in compact mode. Right-click the anchor window to return to full mode. *See also* compact mode.

announcement

> An announcement is a file that contains information about the URL for a media stream, including the multicast IP address, port, stream format, and other station settings. It is a metafile that can be generated automatically by Windows Media Services Administrator when a multicast station is created.

attribute

> A piece of information in the form of a name-value pair that specifies a particular detail of an element in a markup language.

B

bandwidth

The data transfer capacity of a digital communications system, such as the Internet or a local area network (LAN). Bandwidth is usually expressed in the number of bits that a system is capable of transferring in a second: bits per second (bps). High bandwidth or broadband refers to a network capable of a fast data transfer rate.

bit rate

The speed at which digital audio and video content streams from a source, such as a file, to be rendered properly by a player, or the speed at which binary content in general is streamed on a network. Bit rate is usually measured in kilobits per second (Kbps), for example, 28.8 Kbps. The bit rate of a Windows Media file or live stream is determined during the encoding process, when the streaming content is created. Bandwidth is the total bit-rate capacity of a network. For audio and video content to render properly when streaming over a network, the bandwidth of the network must be high enough to accommodate the bit rates of all the different content that is being streamed concurrently.

broadband

A high-speed transmission. The term is commonly used to refer to communications lines or services at T1 rates (1.544 Mbps) *or cable modem rates* and above.

broadcast

Describes how a client experiences receiving a stream. A broadcast stream can be unicast or multicast. In a broadcast connection, the client is passive and does not control when the stream starts or stops. In an on-demand connection, the client is active and controls when the stream is started and stopped.

broadcast multicast

Delivery of one stream by a Windows Media server to many clients. From a client perspective, a broadcast is a connectionless experience because the client never connects to a Windows Media server.

broadcast unicast

A point-to-point connection that a client initiates to a publishing point in a Windows Media server.

buffer

A small amount of RAM that Windows Media Player uses as a loading area for information before playing it. When you play a file or stream, Windows Media Player fills up the buffer before it begins playing so that you won't notice minor problems with traffic on the Internet or the local network.

C

caption

Text that accompanies an image or video stream, either as a supplemental description or a transcript of spoken words.

CD

See compact disc.

client

Typically, the software that makes requests in client/server communications. Client software requests connections and communications with servers. On a local area network or the Internet, a computer that accesses shared network resources provided by another computer (called a server). A computer playing content with Windows Media Player is often called the client.

clipping image

An image that is not displayed, but instead defines the visible region of another image.

codec

Short for compressor/decompressor. Codecs are various types of computer algorithms that are applied to audio, video, and image files to compress the size of the files. The benefit of this is that the files do not use as much disk space when stored or network bandwidth when streamed. To open a compressed file, the same codec must be used to decompress the file. If your computer does not have the correct codec to decompress a file, Windows Media Player will attempt to download the codec for you.

compact mode

Windows Media Player can appear in two modes: full mode or compact mode. Compact mode is the smaller, reduced-functionality mode that is customizable. It allows more room on your screen for using other applications. To make sure you are in compact mode, press CTRL+2.

compact disc (CD)

A small disc containing digital information that is stored or retrieved optically through the use of lasers.

compression

The coding of data to reduce file size or the bit rate of a stream. Content that has been compressed is decompressed for playback.

content

Data that servers stream to a client or clients. Content can originate from live audio or live video presentation, stored audio or video files, still images, or slide shows. The content must be translated from its original state into a Windows Media format before a Windows Media server can stream it. Windows Media servers can stream live streams or stored Window Media files as content.

D

down image

An image that is displayed when the mouse button is in the down position over a control.

download

A method of delivering content over a network in which the content is copied to a client computer and then played locally. This method is different from streaming, because in streaming, the source data is not copied to the client computer. *See also* streaming.

E

element

A unit of information within a markup language that is defined by a tag, or a pair of tags surrounding some content, and includes any attributes defined within the initial tag.

encode

To convert information into a specified digital format for convenient storage and retrieval using computer technology, usually involving compression technology and encryption technology.

error correction

A method of controlling and correcting data transmission errors that occur when streaming.

event

An action that occurs in response to a particular condition within a program, such as a key press or mouse click.

event handler

A method within a program that is called automatically whenever a particular event occurs.

extension

Usually three letters, sometimes more, that are added to the end of a file name. The extension is distinguished from the rest of the file name by a period. The file extension, such as .avi or .txt, usually indicates the file type and the program used to play or open the file. Also known as file extension or file name extension.

F

file format

The structure of a file. *See also* file type; extension;media formats.

file type

Usually indicated by the file name extension. The file type determines which program can be used to play or open a file.

full mode

Windows Media Player can appear in two modes: full mode or compact mode. Full mode is the fully functional mode with complete sets of toolbars. To make sure you are in full mode, press CTRL+1.

G

genre

A category for grouping music, such as "classical" or "jazz".

global attribute

An attribute used within a skin definition file that is accessible from anywhere, rather than being associated with a particular element.

H

hover image

An image that is displayed for a control whenever the mouse pointer hovers over it.

HTTP

Hypertext transfer protocol.

L

licensed file

A Windows Media file that has an associated license restricting the playing of that file. The restrictions stated in the license will vary depending on the license creator. Any file created by copying a CD track using Windows Media Player is assigned a license that restricts the playing of that file to the computer where the file was created.

lossy

An image compression technique that decreases image quality in order to reduce the file size.

M

.mid

A Musical Instrument Digital Interface (MIDI) file. *See also* media formats; MIDI

.midi

A Musical Instrument Digital Interface (MIDI) file. *See also* media formats; MIDI.

.mp2

An MPEG video file. *See also* media formats; Moving Picture Experts Group.

.mp3

An MPEG video file. *See also* media formats; Moving Picture Experts Group.

.mpg

An MPEG video file. *See also* media formats; Moving Picture Experts Group.

.mpg2

An MPEG video file. *See also* media formats; Moving Picture Experts Group.

mapping image

An image that is not displayed, but instead defines significant regions on another image through the use of colors. A mapping image allows arbitrarily complex shapes to be defined easily, without the specification of long lists of coordinates.

media formats
Types of media files. Formats supported by Windows Media Player include the following: .aif, .aifc, .aiff, .asf, .asx, au, .avi, .cda, .ivf, .m1v, .m3u, .mid, .midi, mp2, .mp3, .mpa, .mpe, .mpeg, .mpg, .mpv2, .rmi, .snd, .wax, .wav, .wma, .wms, .wmv, .wvx, .wmz.

metadata
Information about data. For Windows Media Technologies, metadata, such as content title, author, copyright, and description, can be included in a Windows Media file and in a metafile script.

metafile
In Windows Media Technologies, a file that provides information about Windows Media files and their presentation. There are several types of metafiles designated by the following extensions: .asd, .asx, .wax, .wvx, .wmx and .nsc.

metafile playlist
A Window Media metafile that provides information that Windows Media Player uses to receive unicast streams, multicast streams, and other supported media from an intranet or the Internet.

method
A programming function that is related to a particular object and can be called to modify the object's properties or to achieve a particular effect that the object is responsible for. Methods can be passed pieces of information called parameters in order to modify the resulting behavior. Frequently, the result of a method call is the return of a different piece of information that can then be used by another part of the program.

MIDI
See Musical Instrument Digital Interface.

MIME
Multipurpose Internet Mail Extension. It is a multimedia file format that is a standard for multi-part multimedia electronic mail messages and World-Wide Web hypertext documents on the Internet. MIME provides the ability to transfer non-textual data, such as graphics, audio and fax.

Moving Picture Experts Group (MPEG)
There are two major MPEG standards: MPEG-1 and MPEG-2. The most common implementations of the MPEG-1 standard provide a video resolution of 352-by-240 at 30 frames per second (fps). This produces video quality slightly below the quality of conventional VCR videos.

A newer standard, MPEG-2, offers resolutions of 720x480 and 1280x720 at 60 fps, with full CD-quality audio. This is sufficient for all the major TV standards, including NTSC and even HDTV.

MP3
MPEG Audio Layer 3. An audio compression technology that is part of the MPEG-1 and MPEG-2 specifications. Developed in Germany in 1991 by the Fraunhofer Institute, MP3 uses perceptual

audio coding to compress CD-quality sound by a factor of 12, while providing almost the same fidelity.

.mpeg

A Moving Picture Experts Group video file. *See also* media formats; Moving Picture Experts Group.

MPEG-1

See Moving Picture Experts Group.

MPEG-2

See Moving Picture Experts Group.

multicast

A one-to-many client/server connection in which multiple clients receive the same stream from a server. To receive a multicast, a client *listens* to a specific IP address on a multicast-enabled network, like tuning a television to a specific channel. In contrast, a unicast is a one-to-one connection in which each client receives a separate stream from a server.

Musical Instrument Digital Interface (MIDI)

A standard protocol for the interchange of musical information between musical instruments, synthesizers and computers. It defines the codes for a musical event, which include the start of a note, its pitch, length, volume, and musical attributes, such as vibrato. It also defines codes for various button, dial, and pedal adjustments used on synthesizers.

O

object

A collection of properties and methods that serve a particular purpose and are treated as a unit.

P

packet

A small unit of information transmitted over a network.

playlist

A personalized list of links to various audio and video files on your computer, your network, or the Internet, including radio stations and broadband broadcasts. You can create a playlist from any combination of media sources. The items in the list are played sequentially. You can change the order of items in your playlist by dragging and dropping.

port

A number that enables IP packets to be sent to a particular process on a computer connected to a network. Ports are most often identified with a particular service. For example, port 80 on an Internet computer indicates a Web server. Windows Media server components, when in use, bind to particular ports. By default, the Windows Media Unicast service binds to port 1755 and the

Windows Media Station service binds to port 7007. If HTTP streaming is enabled for a service, then that service switches to use port 80.

preset

A predefined setting. For Windows Media Player, there are presets defined for both equalizer settings and for most visualizations.

proxy server

A computer and associated software that will pass on a request for a URL from a browser to an outside server and return the results. This can provide clients that are sealed off from the Internet a trusted agent that can access the Internet on their behalf, or provide a cache of items available on other servers that are presumably slower or more expensive to access.

progress bar

A meter-like indicator within a graphical user interface that illustrates the progress of a gradual process, such as a file download.

property

A piece of information that specifies a particular detail of an object.

protocols

Standard formats and processes for transmitting information over a network. Available protocols for use with streaming media are Multicast, UDP, TCP, and HTTP.

publishing point

A virtual directory used for storing content that is available to clients, or for accessing a live stream. Clients reach a publishing point through its URL.

S

.smi

A Synchronized Accessible Media Interchange (SAMI) file. *See also* Synchronized Accessible Media Interchange (SAMI).

.snd

A UNIX file. *See also* media formats.

SAMI

See Synchronized Accessible Media Interchange (SAMI) File.

skin

A file that customizes the look and functionality of Windows Media Player. When Windows Media Player is in compact mode, it will appear and work as the skin directs.

skin definition file

A text document in XML format that specifies the elements present within a skin, along with their relationships and additional functionality. A skin definition file has a .wms file extension.

slider
A control within a graphical user interface in which an indicator called a thumb can be moved along a continuous path into a number of different positions.

sticky
A characteristic of a button control within a graphical user interface in which the button, when clicked, remains in a down position until it is clicked again. A sticky button is also known as a toggle.

stream
Data transmitted across a network and any properties associated with the data. Streaming is the general term used to describe the method used by Windows Media Services to transmit data to client computers. Specifically, streams can be transmitted as either unicast streams or multicast streams. Streaming data allows the player to begin rendering the data immediately instead of waiting for the entire file to be downloaded.

streaming
A method of delivering content, in which media is located on a server and then played by sending the data across a network in a continuous flow. Streamed media is differentiated from downloaded media because the media is sent in a steady stream to the computer but is not stored on the computer.

Synchronized Accessible Media Interchange (SAMI) File
A file containing text strings associated with specified times within a media presentation. The text strings appear in the Windows Media Player closed captioning display area as the presentation reaches the designated times. SAMI files can also include conditional text strings for providing closed captioning in different languages.

T

tag
A portion of an XML file designated by a pair of angle brackets and the information between them that identifies an element and any of its attributes.

thumb
The part of a slider control that can be moved to set the slider position.

ToolTip
A small text box usually containing help information that pops up when a mouse pointer hovers over a control.

tracks
Individual songs from a CD.

U

Unicode

A universal character encoding standard. A set of uniquely encoded characters of all scripts used by living languages. A text encoded in Unicode consists of a stream of 16-bit Unicode characters without any embedded controls.

UNIX

An interactive, time-sharing operating system. UNIX was the first source-portable operating system and is now offered by many manufacturers.

URL

A Uniform Resource Locator, identifying a protocol, host computer, directory, and file name for the purposes of accessing that file from another computer on a network.

V

video settings

Settings that allow the modification of video brightness, contrast, hue, and saturation.

visualization

Splashes of color and geometric shapes that change with the beat of the audio that is currently playing.

visualization collection

A group of visualizations centered on specific themes.

W

.wav

A Windows audio file. *See also* media formats.

.wax

A Windows Media audio redirector file. A special type of metafile playlist for use with Windows Media files with a .wma extension. The .wax extension file includes information about the location of the .wma file on the Windows Media server and the properties of the file. It is similar to the playlist files with an .asx extension and their interaction with media files with an .asf extension.

See also media formats.

.wma

A Windows Media audio file. A special type of advanced streaming format file for use with audio content encoded with the Windows Media Audio codec. The .wma extension indicates a file format and how the content is encoded.

See also media formats.

.wms

A Windows Media Player skin definition file. A skin definition file is an XML text document that defines the elements present within a skin along with their relationships and functionality. *See also* media formats.

.wmv

A Windows Media video file. *See also* media formats.

.wmz

A Windows Media Player skin file that combines a skin definition file and its supporting graphic files into one file using zip compression technology. *See also* media formats.

.wvx

A Windows Media redirector file. *See also* media formats.

Windows Media client

The ActiveX control, called the Windows Media Player control, that receives and renders content from Windows Media server components. The client can be on the same computer as the server, or it can be on another computer.

Windows Media file

A file, typically with a .wma, or .wmv, or .asf extension, which contains audio, video, or script data. These files are highly optimized for streaming, yet they provide dynamic sound when downloaded and played by Windows Media Player.

Windows Media format

The format used by Microsoft Windows Media Technologies (or a third party product that incorporates a licensed Windows Media technology) to author, store, edit, distribute, stream, or play timeline-based content.

Windows Media Station (.nsc) file

Contains information that Windows Media Player uses to connect to and play a multicast stream, such as the multicast IP address, port, stream format, and other station settings. Unlike a unicast stream, no header information is contained in a multicast stream. That information comes from an .nsc file. Windows Media Player usually opens an announcement (.asx, .wax, or .wvx) file first, that points it to the location of the .nsc file.

X

XML

Extensible Markup Language. A simple dialect of SGML suitable for use on the World-Wide Web and for the creation of custom markup languages such as the Windows Media Player skin definition language.

Index

full mode 25, 137, 155
  changing views 45
Full Mode command 38
Full Screen command 38

G

GIF 129, 161
graphic equalizer 33, 38, 120
  in skins 144
  SRS Wow effects 32
graphics 110, 127, 147
  colors 162
  creating 129, 158
  down images 167, 171
  drawers 189
  hover images 166, 171
  layers 129, 148, 160
  mapping images 164, 171
  sliders 178, 182
  supported file types 128
  transparency 130, 170
  visualizations 186
grayscale 182

H

HEAD element 224
headphones 33
Help 43, 144
Help Topics command 43
hover images 166, 171
HTML
  absolute positioning 226
  DIV element 225, 226, 247
  dynamic HTML 216
  event handlers 227
  forms 223
  HEAD element 224
  IMG element 225
  OBJECT element 222
  PARAM element 222, 247
  SCRIPT element 228

SPAN element 224
TABLE element 225
hue 35
hyperlinks. *See* URL

I

images 110, 127, 147
  colors 162
  creating 129, 158
  down images 167, 171
  drawers 189
  hover images 166, 171
  layers 129, 148, 160
  mapping images 164, 171
  sliders 178, 182
  supported file types 128
  transparency 130, 170
  visualizations 186
IMG element 225
Import Playlist to Library command 37
Indeo video 62, 66
installing
  codecs 41, 69
  new components only 12
  skins 20
  visualizations 22
  Windows Media Player 8

J

Jedor Viscosity 147
JPEG 129, 161
JScript 121, 172, 227
  custom commands 243
  debugging 210
  error messages 205
  Error object 208
  event handlers 202, 203, 245
  events 123, 124, 126
  markers 235
  sample code 192

About the Author

Seth McEvoy has twenty-five years of experience in the computer industry as a programmer and technical writer and editor. He has specialized in learning computer languages, ranging from assembly language to COM to XML and thirty others. In his nine years at Microsoft, he has written the programming code and text for many of their Software Development Kits including: Windows, Office, OLE, and Interactive Television. As a technical editor at Microsoft Press, he edited *Inside OLE,* by Kraig Brockschmidt, and other books.

He has also written 33 computer and children's books for publishers such as Simon & Schuster, Dell, Compute, Bantam, and Random House. One of his children's books, *Not Quite Human*, was adapted for three TV movies by Disney.

MICROSOFT LICENSE AGREEMENT
Book Companion CD

IMPORTANT—READ CAREFULLY: This Microsoft End-User License Agreement ("EULA") is a legal agreement between you (either an individual or an entity) and Microsoft Corporation for the Microsoft product identified above, which includes computer software and may include associated media, printed materials, and "online" or electronic documentation ("SOFTWARE PRODUCT"). Any component included within the SOFTWARE PRODUCT that is accompanied by a separate End-User License Agreement shall be governed by such agreement and not the terms set forth below. By installing, copying, or otherwise using the SOFTWARE PRODUCT, you agree to be bound by the terms of this EULA. If you do not agree to the terms of this EULA, you are not authorized to install, copy, or otherwise use the SOFTWARE PRODUCT; you may, however, return the SOFTWARE PRODUCT, along with all printed materials and other items that form a part of the Microsoft product that includes the SOFTWARE PRODUCT, to the place you obtained them for a full refund.

SOFTWARE PRODUCT LICENSE

The SOFTWARE PRODUCT is protected by United States copyright laws and international copyright treaties, as well as other intellectual property laws and treaties. The SOFTWARE PRODUCT is licensed, not sold.

1. **GRANT OF LICENSE.** This EULA grants you the following rights:

   a. **Software Product.** You may install and use one copy of the SOFTWARE PRODUCT on a single computer. The primary user of the computer on which the SOFTWARE PRODUCT is installed may make a second copy for his or her exclusive use on a portable computer.

   b. **Storage/Network Use.** You may also store or install a copy of the SOFTWARE PRODUCT on a storage device, such as a network server, used only to install or run the SOFTWARE PRODUCT on your other computers over an internal network; however, you must acquire and dedicate a license for each separate computer on which the SOFTWARE PRODUCT is installed or run from the storage device. A license for the SOFTWARE PRODUCT may not be shared or used concurrently on different computers.

   c. **License Pak.** If you have acquired this EULA in a Microsoft License Pak, you may make the number of additional copies of the computer software portion of the SOFTWARE PRODUCT authorized on the printed copy of this EULA, and you may use each copy in the manner specified above. You are also entitled to make a corresponding number of secondary copies for portable computer use as specified above.

   d. **Sample Code.** Solely with respect to portions, if any, of the SOFTWARE PRODUCT that are identified within the SOFTWARE PRODUCT as sample code (the "SAMPLE CODE"):

      i. **Use and Modification.** Microsoft grants you the right to use and modify the source code version of the SAMPLE CODE, *provided* you comply with subsection (d)(iii) below. You may not distribute the SAMPLE CODE, or any modified version of the SAMPLE CODE, in source code form.

      ii. **Redistributable Files.** Provided you comply with subsection (d)(iii) below, Microsoft grants you a nonexclusive, royalty-free right to reproduce and distribute the object code version of the SAMPLE CODE and of any modified SAMPLE CODE, other than SAMPLE CODE, or any modified version thereof, designated as not redistributable in the Readme file that forms a part of the SOFTWARE PRODUCT (the "Non-Redistributable Sample Code"). All SAMPLE CODE other than the Non-Redistributable Sample Code is collectively referred to as the "REDISTRIBUTABLES."

      iii. **Redistribution Requirements.** If you redistribute the REDISTRIBUTABLES, you agree to: (i) distribute the REDISTRIBUTABLES in object code form only in conjunction with and as a part of your software application product; (ii) not use Microsoft's name, logo, or trademarks to market your software application product; (iii) include a valid copyright notice on your software application product; (iv) indemnify, hold harmless, and defend Microsoft from and against any claims or lawsuits, including attorney's fees, that arise or result from the use or distribution of your software application product; and (v) not permit further distribution of the REDISTRIBUTABLES by your end user. Contact Microsoft for the applicable royalties due and other licensing terms for all other uses and/or distribution of the REDISTRIBUTABLES.

2. **DESCRIPTION OF OTHER RIGHTS AND LIMITATIONS.**

   - **Limitations on Reverse Engineering, Decompilation, and Disassembly.** You may not reverse engineer, decompile, or disassemble the SOFTWARE PRODUCT, except and only to the extent that such activity is expressly permitted by applicable law notwithstanding this limitation.

   - **Separation of Components.** The SOFTWARE PRODUCT is licensed as a single product. Its component parts may not be separated for use on more than one computer.

   - **Rental.** You may not rent, lease, or lend the SOFTWARE PRODUCT.

- **Support Services.** Microsoft may, but is not obligated to, provide you with support services related to the SOFTWARE PRODUCT ("Support Services"). Use of Support Services is governed by the Microsoft policies and programs described in the user manual, in "online" documentation, and/or in other Microsoft-provided materials. Any supplemental software code provided to you as part of the Support Services shall be considered part of the SOFTWARE PRODUCT and subject to the terms and conditions of this EULA. With respect to technical information you provide to Microsoft as part of the Support Services, Microsoft may use such information for its business purposes, including for product support and development. Microsoft will not utilize such technical information in a form that personally identifies you.

- **Software Transfer.** You may permanently transfer all of your rights under this EULA, provided you retain no copies, you transfer all of the SOFTWARE PRODUCT (including all component parts, the media and printed materials, any upgrades, this EULA, and, if applicable, the Certificate of Authenticity), **and** the recipient agrees to the terms of this EULA.

- **Termination.** Without prejudice to any other rights, Microsoft may terminate this EULA if you fail to comply with the terms and conditions of this EULA. In such event, you must destroy all copies of the SOFTWARE PRODUCT and all of its component parts.

3. **COPYRIGHT.** All title and copyrights in and to the SOFTWARE PRODUCT (including but not limited to any images, photographs, animations, video, audio, music, text, SAMPLE CODE, REDISTRIBUTABLES, and "applets" incorporated into the SOFTWARE PRODUCT) and any copies of the SOFTWARE PRODUCT are owned by Microsoft or its suppliers. The SOFTWARE PRODUCT is protected by copyright laws and international treaty provisions. Therefore, you must treat the SOFTWARE PRODUCT like any other copyrighted material **except** that you may install the SOFTWARE PRODUCT on a single computer provided you keep the original solely for backup or archival purposes. You may not copy the printed materials accompanying the SOFTWARE PRODUCT.

4. **U.S. GOVERNMENT RESTRICTED RIGHTS.** The SOFTWARE PRODUCT and documentation are provided with RESTRICTED RIGHTS. Use, duplication, or disclosure by the Government is subject to restrictions as set forth in subparagraph (c)(1)(ii) of the Rights in Technical Data and Computer Software clause at DFARS 252.227-7013 or subparagraphs (c)(1) and (2) of the Commercial Computer Software—Restricted Rights at 48 CFR 52.227-19, as applicable. Manufacturer is Microsoft Corporation/One Microsoft Way/Redmond, WA 98052-6399.

5. **EXPORT RESTRICTIONS.** You agree that you will not export or re-export the SOFTWARE PRODUCT, any part thereof, or any process or service that is the direct product of the SOFTWARE PRODUCT (the foregoing collectively referred to as the "Restricted Components"), to any country, person, entity, or end user subject to U.S. export restrictions. You specifically agree not to export or re-export any of the Restricted Components (i) to any country to which the U.S. has embargoed or restricted the export of goods or services, which currently include, but are not necessarily limited to, Cuba, Iran, Iraq, Libya, North Korea, Sudan, and Syria, or to any national of any such country, wherever located, who intends to transmit or transport the Restricted Components back to such country; (ii) to any end user who you know or have reason to know will utilize the Restricted Components in the design, development, or production of nuclear, chemical, or biological weapons; or (iii) to any end user who has been prohibited from participating in U.S. export transactions by any federal agency of the U.S. government. You warrant and represent that neither the BXA nor any other U.S. federal agency has suspended, revoked, or denied your export privileges.

DISCLAIMER OF WARRANTY

NO WARRANTIES OR CONDITIONS. MICROSOFT EXPRESSLY DISCLAIMS ANY WARRANTY OR CONDITION FOR THE SOFTWARE PRODUCT. THE SOFTWARE PRODUCT AND ANY RELATED DOCUMENTATION ARE PROVIDED "AS IS" WITHOUT WARRANTY OR CONDITION OF ANY KIND, EITHER EXPRESS OR IMPLIED, INCLUDING, WITHOUT LIMITATION, THE IMPLIED WARRANTIES OF MERCHANTABILITY, FITNESS FOR A PARTICULAR PURPOSE, OR NONINFRINGEMENT. THE ENTIRE RISK ARISING OUT OF USE OR PERFORMANCE OF THE SOFTWARE PRODUCT REMAINS WITH YOU.

LIMITATION OF LIABILITY. TO THE MAXIMUM EXTENT PERMITTED BY APPLICABLE LAW, IN NO EVENT SHALL MICROSOFT OR ITS SUPPLIERS BE LIABLE FOR ANY SPECIAL, INCIDENTAL, INDIRECT, OR CONSEQUENTIAL DAMAGES WHATSOEVER (INCLUDING, WITHOUT LIMITATION, DAMAGES FOR LOSS OF BUSINESS PROFITS, BUSINESS INTERRUPTION, LOSS OF BUSINESS INFORMATION, OR ANY OTHER PECUNIARY LOSS) ARISING OUT OF THE USE OF OR INABILITY TO USE THE SOFTWARE PRODUCT OR THE PROVISION OF OR FAILURE TO PROVIDE SUPPORT SERVICES, EVEN IF MICROSOFT HAS BEEN ADVISED OF THE POSSIBILITY OF SUCH DAMAGES. IN ANY CASE, MICROSOFT'S ENTIRE LIABILITY UNDER ANY PROVISION OF THIS EULA SHALL BE LIMITED TO THE GREATER OF THE AMOUNT ACTUALLY PAID BY YOU FOR THE SOFTWARE PRODUCT OR US$5.00; PROVIDED, HOWEVER, IF YOU HAVE ENTERED INTO A MICROSOFT SUPPORT SERVICES AGREEMENT, MICROSOFT'S ENTIRE LIABILITY REGARDING SUPPORT SERVICES SHALL BE GOVERNED BY THE TERMS OF THAT AGREEMENT. BECAUSE SOME STATES AND JURISDICTIONS DO NOT ALLOW THE EXCLUSION OR LIMITATION OF LIABILITY, THE ABOVE LIMITATION MAY NOT APPLY TO YOU.

MISCELLANEOUS

This EULA is governed by the laws of the State of Washington USA, except and only to the extent that applicable law mandates governing law of a different jurisdiction.

Should you have any questions concerning this EULA, or if you desire to contact Microsoft for any reason, please contact the Microsoft subsidiary serving your country, or write: Microsoft Sales Information Center/One Microsoft Way/Redmond, WA 98052-6399.

OWNER REGISTRATION CARD   *Register Today!*   0-7356-1178-5

Return the bottom portion of this card to register today.

Microsoft® Windows Media™ Player 7 Handbook

FIRST NAME   MIDDLE INITIAL   LAST NAME

INSTITUTION OR COMPANY NAME

ADDRESS

CITY   STATE   ZIP

(   )

E-MAIL ADDRESS   PHONE NUMBER

U.S. and Canada addresses only. Fill in information above and mail postage-free.
Please mail only the bottom half of this page.

**For information about Microsoft Press®
products, visit our Web site at
mspress.microsoft.com**

Microsoft®